CW00493596

A Bridge to
Recovery

A Bridge to
Recovery

A Guide to Life Care Planning
& Finding Your Way Back
After Trauma

SANTO STEVEN BIFULCO, MD, CLCP

LIONCREST
PUBLISHING

A Bridge to Recovery
A Guide to Life Care Planning & Finding Your Way Back After Trauma

ISBN 978-1-5445-2330-9 *Hardcover*
       978-1-5445-2328-6 *Paperback*
       978-1-5445-2329-3 *Ebook*
       978-1-5445-2331-6 *Audiobook*

In no particular order...

*To my very grand daughter, **Brianna**,*
whose love is unconditional and amazing.
You give me a reason to fight and wake up every day.

*To my youngest of four, **Dominic Santo**,*
*my oldest daughter, **Angelina Carmela**,*
*and my oldest son, **Santo Philip**,*
you each have inspired and taught me
more than you can ever know.

To my wonderful and beautiful spouse
and life and business partner,
***Cynthia Elizabeth Landeta BiFulco**.*

To my youngest (of six siblings)
*brother, **Phil**; my younger sister, **Linda Doremus**;*
*my big brother, **Jerry**; my big sister, **Louise Horne**; and **Gerry**.*

*To my mother, **Michelina**, and my father, **Phil**.*

*To my Nanos, **Santo Accurso** and **Gerard BiFulco**.*

*To my mother and father-in-law, **Zorida** and **Philip Landeta**.*

*To my best friend, **Andrew.***

To my teams, including those who
have been with me through this journey:
***Bethany**, **Allison**, **Alexis**, **Philip**, and **Claudia**.*

To my mentors, you know who you are
and how much I love and appreciate you.
*Special mention to **Bill Anton**, **Ron Fleisher**,*
*and **Charles "Red" Scott**.*

To my publisher.

You each should know that words cannot express
the gratitude and love I have for each of you.
This book would not have been written
if it were not for you.

CONTENTS

PREFACE

Let me first say that I don't know much relative to what I need to know. Whatever success I've had in my life has more to do with me knowing how to deal with my not knowing than knowing.

It's presumptuous that I should be telling anyone what to do if you were to ask me. But I'm going to share what I know and my story so that others may benefit. I believe that by sharing what I know and what I've learned, it may help others. I certainly hope it will.

Success for me would be a single life changed or improved as a result of this book. I'm at a stage of my life where it's much more important to me to pass on what I've learned about how to be successful than to actually have or seek more material success for myself.

What you choose to do with this knowledge, my story, and these principles is up to you. I believe you have to be an independent thinker and make choices for yourself based on your own values. Ask yourself, "What is true?"

The knowledge I'm going to share with you came from a lifetime of making mistakes and reflecting on those mistakes. And the truth is I'm still making mistakes all the time.

This book is for anyone whose life has been impacted by trauma. This includes victims of accidents, illness, and birth injuries; it also includes friends and family of trauma survivors, as well as physicians and attorneys.

People who have suffered a traumatic injury often feel trapped in the darkness of a new life they didn't ask for. They need to know how to emerge from trauma to a better life. This book is designed as a resource and roadmap for that recovery: physically, mentally, emotionally, and spiritually. Regardless of where YOU are. It is my hope that by the end of these pages you will have a better understanding of how to deal with and manage the impact of physical pain and psychological struggles, secure financial resources, and adjust to a new way of life. Please understand that while your life may not return to exactly the way it was before your injury, you can absolutely live with less pain, more happiness, and a better overall quality of life than today.

If you're the friend or family member of a trauma victim, I hope this book provides you with some knowledge and insight about what your loved one is going through—the immense physical and emotional challenges. Also, you will find recommended resources to enhance your understanding of trauma and life care planning that could prove incredibly beneficial.

Physicians can benefit greatly from this book because it shows what it's like to be on the other side of trauma. I am not only a life care planner, but I have also been a successful, practicing rehabilitation physician for many years, more than three decades in fact. Perhaps most critically, I have suffered trauma. A whole new world of understanding opened up to me when I was laying on the examination table rather than performing the evaluation.

Lastly, I have written this book with the intention of providing a valuable resource to plaintiff and defense attorneys to hand off to their personal injury litigation clients. Both plaintiff and defense lawyers will find here a wealth of information about not only understanding trauma better, but laying out the basics and benefits of a well-documented physician-authored life care plan. From an attorney's perspective, this book will also provide invaluable knowledge about what their clients should expect in a litigation process. Both parties will be better prepared for litigation simply by absorbing the content within these pages.

After reading this book you need to decide for yourself what to do and what is true for you. And you will need to have the courage to do it. It's been said that time is like a river that carries us forward into encounters with reality that require us to make decisions. I hope your decision to pick up this book turns out to be a good one.

INTRODUCTION

*"Life isn't about waiting for
the storm to pass, it's about learning
how to dance in the rain."*

—Vivian Greene (author)

Every year, millions of Americans suffer traumatic injuries. I am one of them, and I'm deeply sorry if you can relate. If you're looking for answers after going through this type of experience, you're not alone, although I know it might feel that way.

This book is written for anyone whose life has changed because of unexpected trauma. It's also intended to be a guide for those whose loved ones have undergone this kind of life-altering experience. Perhaps this trauma was unexpected and its results immediate. For example, maybe you were in an accident or otherwise suffered at the hands of someone else's negligence. Or maybe you suffered from this kind of trauma, but the ramifications did not immediately present themselves as a serious threat to your quality of life. It was only later on that you realized the injury you sustained would forever change the way you live. Either way, this experience might have caused you to incur permanent losses—physically, psychologically, vocationally, or socially. Now you need answers to questions about what your recovery looks like and how you will acquire the necessary resources to make that recovery happen in the best way.

You likely now find yourself lost in the darkness of fear and uncertainty. You feel trapped in a reality you never asked for—one in which every day requires you to manage extreme physical challenges, not to mention a myriad of difficult and complex emotions. At least, that's how I felt after my injury.

Only after my mindset shifted from anger and bitterness to gratitude and determination did I arrive at a much better place. That's what led me to find the assistance of a few special medical professionals, as well as a new direction for my career, one that is geared toward helping others who find themselves in the same situation I was in. Even if your situation is much worse than mine was, which included a variety of physical injuries and a mild traumatic brain injury (mTBI). This book can help you to live a much happier, more fulfilled existence.

Perhaps a good place to start is to tell you who I am, what I do, and all about my experience with trauma.

AN MD, CLCP (CERTIFIED LIFE CARE PLANNER), AND SURVIVOR OF AN MTBI (MILD TRAUMATIC BRAIN INJURY)

My name is Santo Steven BiFulco. I received my medical degree from the University of South Florida College of Medicine in Tampa, Florida, and completed my residency in physical medicine and rehabilitation at Nassau County Medical Center in East Meadow, New York.

I began my private practice as a rehabilitation physician in 1990, specializing in the treatment of chronic disabling musculoskeletal, orthopedic, and neurological disorders.

Many of my patients came to me with intolerable acute and chronic pain. Although I always made a sincere effort to listen to their needs, I couldn't possibly have understood the magnitude of what they were going through, until years later when I became a patient myself.

My life changed forever one night in mid-December 1999. At the time, my marriage of thirteen years was in a state of conflict, which caused me to have restless bouts of insomnia. Most nights, I fell asleep as early as 9:00 p.m., only to wake up a few hours later. On this particular night, I decided that 3:00 a.m. was the perfect time to move my Jet Ski a few miles from our house to our condo. I still have no idea why that urge came over me at that time.

Fully awake and ready to get things done, I hitched the Jet Ski up to the back of my Jeep and pulled out of our neighborhood. A few minutes later, I stopped to take a left turn from the turning lane of a four-lane divided highway. Of course, there were very few cars on the road at this hour, but I noticed a pair of headlights in the distance, weaving wildly from one side of the road to the other.

It's strange how slowly time seems to pass in life's most pivotal moments. Although the car was coming pretty fast, I still had time to consider my options. My first thought was that the driver was probably coming home from a holiday party and severely impaired. I considered hitting the gas hard to make my left turn as quickly as possible and get the heck out of his way. Unfortunately, with that Jet Ski in tow, such an evasive maneuver seemed nearly impossible to make in time, so I really had no other choice but to wait.

As the car got closer, I hoped to be lucky enough that the driver would weave around me, instead of through me. As it turns out, luck was not on my side that night. The car hit me head-on.

The crash itself seemed like a slow-motion movie sequence, but when it was over, everything moved quite fast. I was stunned but fully conscious. I looked around and realized that, luckily, I was okay. Surely I had some injuries, but nothing seemed too far out of place, so I got out of my car and tried to figure out what to do next. The driver of the other vehicle also got out of his car. His objective, it turns out, was to argue with me about how *I* had caused the accident. He didn't get far into his speech before he fell facedown on the pavement in a drunken stupor.

Luckily, an off-duty officer from a local sheriff's department witnessed the accident and its aftermath. He picked the guy up and tried to get him to sit inside of his car to calm down, but the drunk driver took offense and acted belligerently. The off-duty officer called for assistance and waited until a tow truck, ambulance, and his fellow officers arrived on the scene.

The police gave the guy a field sobriety test and he failed, so they took him away in handcuffs. I felt shaken up, but not incapacitated, so I declined transport to a hospital. There was some pain, but it wasn't that bad yet, probably because I was still in a state of shock. I told the paramedics that I was fine and I insisted on walking home. A bit battered and bruised, I trekked back to my house and got ready to go to work. At the time, I didn't realize this was a big mistake.

That workday was physically painful, mentally taxing, and vastly unproductive. After a few hours, my body let me know there was much more wrong with me than I had initially believed.

Remember how I said there are two groups of people for which this book was written? I am part of that second group: the group that sustains trauma without immediately realizing the impact it will have on their lives. In the immediate wake of the crash, I never imagined that my life was about to start spiraling downhill.

I walked around the office that first day with a horrible headache, a stiff neck, an aching back the likes of which I had never experienced before, and a strange numbness in my left hand. The pain in my back was particularly bothersome. It started on the left side, around the middle of my back. At first, it felt like someone's thumb was pressing down hard on me. Within a short amount of time, it felt more like a hot knife cutting through the entirety of my back.

The pain became so intense that I couldn't properly focus on anything else. If I was talking to a patient, my attention was divided between listening to them and gritting my teeth through the increasing pain in my back. If a staff member approached me with a problem, I projected my pain onto them by reacting with impatience.

Unfortunately, that pain didn't just last for the duration of that day, nor was it limited to that week or even the next several months.

In addition to managing chronic pain, my thoughts were foggy and my memory and recall were not as sharp as I was accustomed to. Whether it was the distraction of the pain or another problem I wasn't yet aware of, people around me were pointing out that I was forgetting basic routines and skipping standard processes and procedures. That became incredibly frustrating.

I had always taken pride in being conscientious. At that time of my life, I was not only a devoted husband, loving father, and practicing physician, but also a student pilot on my way to becoming a helicopter operator. I was in charge of a large medical practice and managed many employees. In the wake of my injury, keeping all of those balls in the air became nearly impossible. I began to wonder what my identity would become if I could no longer fulfill those roles and responsibilities.

Losing my grip on all of those things I'd always been able to do well began to overwhelm my mind, but that wasn't my only worry. To make matters worse, my father was diagnosed with terminal cancer and my ability to attend to marital conflict diminished, ultimately leading to the demise of my marriage. Life was proceeding, but my ability to manage it was impaired.

Through my own experience and those of many patients I've spoken with, I've learned that serious trouble usually comes in bunches. That was definitely the case for me, as I found myself fighting a storm of problems on several fronts in my life.

With work becoming more of a struggle every day, I decided that it might be a good idea to delegate some of my responsibilities to the people around me. In the wake of my father's diagnosis, I began to spend more time with him and my family in South Florida. I knew his pancreatic cancer did *not* give him good odds for survival. Sadly, I was proven correct not too long after my visit. His death hit me and my family hard, and it only compounded the multitude of challenges I was dealing with at the time.

The challenges I faced after my injury did not relent; they were merciless. It turns out that pain and stress don't take it easy on you just because you've encountered another tragedy. If anything, they are exacerbated, perhaps because of your impaired ability to deal with them. Although I continued to work, I began lessening my workload and the pain was as intense as ever.

When I finally realized that I was suffering from something more serious than just a few bumps and bruises, I went to see my trusted colleagues—those whom I would normally refer my patients to—for a diagnosis. The news was a little more alarming than I thought it would be. My diagnoses included: nerve injuries in my back and arm, disc injuries, and an mTBI, which is a ridiculous term because there's no such thing as *mild* when it comes to brain injuries. Nonetheless, these are the terms used in medicine.

Before my injury, most people would have described me as gregarious and easygoing. Life wasn't good; it was great! I had a beautiful family, a flourishing medical practice, material success, and an abundance of personal fulfillment. The struggles I was facing as a result of my injury stole all of that. Even worse, the effects of these injuries were taking my joy for life away and turning me into a different person.

The new me experienced emotions that weren't common prior to my injury—things like bitterness, anger, and depression. I became short-tempered with my staff and, most regrettably, with my family. I stopped laughing as much as I had before. I didn't want to socialize, and I gradually watched everything around me begin to change. My world became darker.

More than anything, I felt frustrated and confused. I refused to accept that my life was never going to get any better. Maybe it was sheer stubbornness, but I refused to stay angry and bitter. I continued wishing, hoping, and praying that the new state of my body and mind would go away. After a while, however, I began to run out of options.

BETTER DAYS AHEAD

This new state of frustration, confusion, and pain lasted a long time. I could stay angry and bitter, or I could start doing things differently. It was clear that just going to doctors and attending therapy wasn't enough to help. I had to make the decision that I'd hit bottom. I could either be complacent and stay there or get up and move again. That decision didn't take days or weeks for me; it took years.

As a physical medicine and rehabilitation specialist, I had worked with trauma-related injuries throughout my career. Many of my patients had enlisted the services of non-physician life care planners. These professionals interviewed their clients' treating physicians, to find out exactly what medical intervention their clients would need after a traumatic incident and what those resources would cost over a lifetime. I decided to take a cue from my clients and do the same.

After working with a few life care planners and seeing the difference a well-crafted life care plan (LCP) made in the quality of life for my patients, I realized life care planning wasn't just a healthcare nuance, but *a must-have for anyone who has suffered a life-changing trauma.*

Looking back from my vantage point today, twenty years after my accident, I can see that my injury served as a catalyst for me to switch professional gears.

"Who's more equipped to be a life care planner," I wondered, "than a rehabilitation physician with years of experience working with trauma?" The decision to become a life care planner energized me in a way I hadn't felt in decades. Not since well before my accident had I felt like I was on the verge of something so new and exciting.

Determined to turn what happened to me years prior into something positive, I became a Certified Life Care Planner (CLCP). Since then, I've worked with and continue to work with clients to create life care plans that answer important questions and help individuals discover their bridge to recovery and acquire the resources they need to cross it.

I would never wish the pain and anguish I felt for so long in the wake of my accident on even my worst enemy. But I can't change what happened, and neither can you. What you *can* change is what you do in this moment and moving forward. Unfortunately, I know there are many people who have suffered fates far worse than mine; people who have become paralyzed, incurred permanent brain damage, or slipped into a coma.

Regardless of your injury, you have choices, some of which can make things better for you than they are right now. Your life might never look or feel exactly like it did before your trauma (mine doesn't), but life can be *better* than what you think is possible today.

It all starts by building that bridge and creating your life care plan.

PART I

Managing Your Trauma

Chapter 1

First Steps to Recovery

*"Today is a brand-new day:
a day to heal, a day to love, a day to forgive,
a day to encourage, a day to start afresh."*

—Caroline Naoroji (author)

If you're reading this as the survivor of a traumatic injury, your life has probably changed infirst-line unimaginable ways. Your career and social life are likely a glimmer of what they once were. People treat you differently than they once did, and activities you once enjoyed may no longer be possible. Questions about your future consume your every thought, day and night. It feels like darkness has descended upon you.

I found myself in a similar position after my accident, and I guarantee you that even if your situation is far worse than mine was, there is a path out of the darkness. The first step is to ask yourself an important question:

Why do I want to get better?

Discovering your why will lead you down the path to other answers that provide peace of mind and healing. Life is full of reasons to exist with less pain, anxiety, and emotional turmoil. Even if you're reading this from a massively reduced physical and/or psychological state, *better is still possible.*

Better could mean reducing your pain from a nine and a half on the pain scale to a six, or maybe less.

Better could mean using prayer or meditation to achieve a more peaceful state of mind.

Better could mean rediscovering how to perform one simple activity that you took for granted before your accident.

Better could mean transforming a negative vision of the future into a positive one.

Better could mean something different for everybody. For me, it was *my relationship with my children.*

Growing up, I was blessed with outstanding parents, grandparents, and siblings. My family was strong and supportive. In many ways, my childhood fit the mold of the American dream. Yet, I realized that I was putting my kids in a vastly different situation.

Rather than providing them with the same idyllic childhood, I put them on the path of a broken home. Furthermore, my injury had given them a father with a broken body, but more importantly a broken state of mind.

I knew what a good father looked like, because I had one. But I wasn't fitting the bill myself. I suppose most of us strive to live up to the image of our parents in one way or another. I knew I had big changes to make to achieve that. So, I became determined to do better, not just for myself, but for my kids as well. They were my *why*.

WHY DO YOU WANT TO RECOVER?

Before you read any further, it's important to at least start considering what your *why* is. You don't need to decide now, but think about the possibilities.

Think about how you can reduce pain and anxiety.

Think about how you can heal relationships.

Think about possibilities for a career change.

Start thinking about all the reasons to create a more positive future.

Your life may never get back to the way it was before, but it can get better than it is today.

After you've begun exploring why you want to feel better, get educated about your injury. This will help you get from knowing why you want to recover to taking actual steps in that recovery process.

If your end goal is to recover because you want to be a better parent, educating yourself about your injury will provide answers about how you can overcome specific problems that are currently inhibiting your ability to do that.

Learn everything you can about your situation. Read books, search the internet, and above all, ask questions. Your healthcare team should be built to provide answers. Find out what their short-term and long-term plan is for your care, how various procedures will help you, what technology is available or may become available, what the effects of your medications will be, and more. Keep a curious mind about everything concerning your injury.

Unfortunately, some doctors prefer *not* to give their opinions about future care over the course of a patient's lifetime. Some physicians aren't used to thinking that way, and every patient's situation is different. Predicting the need for care in ten, twenty, thirty years or more can be difficult.

Chances are you have several specialists. This might include a primary care physician, visiting nurses, therapists, attorneys, highly involved family members and friends, and perhaps several others who all have input into your daily care. Being able to ask any or all of them questions when needed is wonderful. However, a central resource who coordinates with all of these caregivers and communicates their thoughts to you is invaluable.

WHAT IS A LIFE CARE PLAN?

Build your team of healthcare professionals and make improvements whenever necessary. They can help you find answers about your why and how you recover. While building that team, enlist the services of a life care planner. That person can be the central point of contact that brings the team together and communicates back to you, in plain English, the answers you need to enhance your education about your injury. Furthermore, the life care plan that person drafts will act as a roadmap for yourself and your team to refer back to throughout the rest of your life.

Beyond the security of having a roadmap for your recovery, the life care planner most importantly provides trauma victims with a document that provides the single source of truth in a deposition or trial setting to determine the allocation of necessary financial resources to make the individual whole again.

One Chance Only

In personal injury law, you get one chance at justice. If you undervalue your injuries in court or in a settlement, you will not have the opportunity to revisit the process and collect further damages.

Life care planners are trained to seize this one-time chance at monetary damages. They work extensively with your healthcare team and others to provide a detailed and comprehensive report (often thousands of pages) to ensure all your needs will be accounted for in the immediate and long-term future.

Origins

In 1981, Dr. Scott Raffa published a document called *Damages in Tort Actions.* His work set forth the guidelines for determining civil litigation damages in personal injury cases. It also served as a long overdue introduction of life care planning to the healthcare industry.

Four years later, Dr. Paul Deutsch wrote *A Guide to Rehabilitation.* This publication expanded the field to a much bigger audience, including the United States. These works hold up as gold standards within the industry. The authors addressed a critical need within the healthcare system, which was a document that would hold up in court to let all parties know what a trauma survivor needs to recover as much as possible.

A Formal Definition

Dr. Deutsch defines the life care plan as "a dynamic document based upon published standards of practice, comprehensive assessment, data analysis, and research, which provides an organized, concise plan for current and future needs with associated costs for individuals who have experienced catastrophic injury or have chronic healthcare needs."

Scientific Foundation

A life care plan considers a voluminous amount of data regarding medical devices, medications, imaging studies, diagnostic tests, treatment plans, injections, surgeries, future appointments, home care, and whatever else your healthcare team deems necessary for your best recovery. Your planner will then crunch the numbers and come up with a dollar figure that represents the total damages due to you.

Often, an economist will assist in this process. This person will conduct a thorough economic analysis that factors in the rising costs of equipment and services, as well as inflation over a patient's life expectancy. Additional professionals may also be brought in, depending on the individual case. No stone should be left unturned in a professionally crafted life care plan.

The life care plan provides the single source of truth in any pending litigation; it answers many questions for all interested parties, including your attorney, treating physicians, expert witnesses, the defense attorney, and anyone else who needs to know the facts surrounding your case.

Scientific foundation must provide the base of the conclusions within the life care plan. Medical professionals must provide the facts about a patient's case, and there can be zero ambiguity, meaning credibility and transparency are at the heart of the document.

Credibility is evident when the patient's physician is licensed and qualified to provide knowledgeable recommendations based on scientific principle.

Transparency means all the necessary data to prove the requirements for care is made available in the document, and there can be no question about its validity. Liability must also come only from a traumatic, injury-causing event.

No preexisting condition can be accounted for in a life care plan. Damages cannot be awarded for injuries or illnesses that weren't directly caused by an act of someone else's negligence. When the possibility for an overlap exists between a traumatic event and a preexisting condition, the life care planner should take great care in trying to separate the two issues and arrive at a reasonable conclusion that will pass legal scrutiny.

Daubert Motion

If an attorney (defense or plaintiff attorney) thinks the life care plan should not be allowed in court, they can file a

Daubert motion. This would result in a hearing, where the underlying reasoning and methodology of the document would be challenged and scrutinized for validity and admissibility.

Certification

What began as a niche practice within the healthcare industry is now becoming a widespread practice, with an abundance of qualified life care planners ready to work with patients who need them.

Many noncertified life care planners are available and I'm sure they're skilled and worthy of working on your case. There is also a certification process, however, for medical professionals and others willing to study hard and obtain the moniker of a Certified Life Care Planner (CLCP). If a person happens to be a physician, they can apply to be a Certified Physician Life Care Planner (CPLCP). My certification is governed by the International Commission on Healthcare Certification (ICHCC).

A prerequisite for certification is that the applicant must already be working in a related industry, in a capacity such as a medical doctor (MD), registered nurse (RN), rehabilitation physician, occupational or physical therapist, attorney, social worker, psychologist, or physician's assistant.

The certification process is exhaustive. It requires 120 hours of training, followed by a rigorous board examination. Furthermore, applicants need to recertify every five years. These requirements ensure that certified life care planners remain updated on the latest medical advances and changes in law that periodically occur.

Certification may not be the only determining factor in a great life care planner, but it is an excellent way to ensure you're working with someone who is willing to work hard to be exemplary in their craft and stay up to date on the latest medical advances, legal requirements, and other specifications and procedures.

Getting Started

Thinking about a life care plan probably isn't at the front of your mind right now. Let's face facts—you have other things to worry about.

The fact is, the sooner you get started on writing a life care plan, the sooner you can at least relieve the burden of wondering how you're going to pay off your medical bills. Not only that, but getting your life care plan written as early as possible will help you to chart your healing progress. Psychologically, you'll achieve the peace of mind that comes from knowing the terrain of the road ahead. You'll start to recognize milestones on your journey to a better day, and understand the progress you're making.

Lastly, getting started on your life care plan as soon as possible will document dates and times of services, which will come in handy if and when there is a deposition or in a trial setting.

You should be an active contributor in your life care planning process, but whoever you hire—certified or not—will guide you through every step of the process.

The life care plan focuses on the dollar figure related to your medical costs from the date of your injury to the end of life only; it does *not* include hedonic damages, which is a dollar figure associated with the loss of enjoyment of life. The LCP also does not include lost capacity for earnings. Those are separate dollar figures—related to *pain and suffering*—that are combined with medical costs to form a total dollar value to your litigation case. However, this document also highlights the complexity of your injury for the purposes of litigation; it describes exactly what you need to do as a result of your new physical and psychological state.

Recommended Resource

A Physician's Guide to Life Care Planning, published by
the American Academy of Physician Life Care Planners and
written by Joe Gonzales MD, is a great way to educate
yourself on life care planning.

Dr. Gonzales's work is an excellent resource for anyone
enlisting the services of a life care planner. No medical
degree is required for this reading. In fact, the book is written
in plain language so just about anyone can grasp it on the
first read.

BETTER DAYS AHEAD

Since becoming a CLPC, I've seen so many instances of a life
care plan making an enormous difference in the quality of
someone's life.

Many years ago, I was the life care planner for a client who
had a bullet from a misfire at a gun range lodged into his liver.
Apparently, the angle at which the bullet was stuck in the liver
made it too dangerous to remove. As a result, the lead from the

bullet was slowly being released into this person's body, causing debilitating and potentially deadly lead poisoning.

Fortunately, there was a medical process capable of helping this person. Not long ago, there would have been no course of action to prolong this person's life. Today, heavy metals stuck in the body can be counteracted by a process called chelation therapy. With that treatment, this patient would eventually be able to recover most of his lost abilities from the accident. So, chelation therapy to the rescue for this person, right? Well, it wasn't that simple. Someone had to pay for the procedure. This patient had no way of covering the costs, so he needed to collect damages based on the fact that someone else was liable for his injury.

This person enlisted my services as a life care planner. We wrote an amount of damages into the plan that would cover this life-sustaining treatment. By spelling out the exact therapy needed, the benefit to the patient, and the anticipated result without this treatment, the document stood up in deposition and secured the payment for his life-saving treatment.

Before the life care plan became a tool for trauma victims, it was extremely challenging to collect the necessary funds to pay for treatments like this one, and other treatments related to brain injuries, severe burns, electrical injuries, birth injuries, multitrauma, and others.

Each form of trauma brings with it a unique set of goals and objectives for the life care plan. The plan should be designed to address your *exact* needs. Every person's situation is different, so there is no template to follow. You and your life care planner will collaborate closely to ensure the best results for your unique circumstances.

Throughout this book, you'll read about cases related to many of the forms of trauma that I've worked with over the years. The point is not only to highlight the necessity of a life care plan for those who have suffered trauma, but also to demonstrate what's possible for recovery. Many of the people I discuss in these stories have emerged from total darkness into a much better and brighter day.

Recommended Resource

Life Care Planning and Case Management Handbook by Roger Weed and Debra Berens is another excellent way to learn about the basics and the details of a life care plan.

Chapter 2

Understanding Brain Injuries

"Acceptance doesn't mean resignation;
it means understanding that something is what it is
and that there has got to be a way through it."

—Michael J. Fox (actor)

What did you love to do before your injury? Did you play racquetball? What about volunteer work? Participate in a social club? How about skiing, swimming, or running? Maybe you enjoyed walking the dog in the park every day. We all have activities and pastimes that add joy to our lives. Things that define us, make us.

When an injury takes those things away, life becomes less joyous, and there is a tendency to resist or complain about the involuntary loss in our lives. Chances are, if you've suffered a traumatic injury, you've lost something that used to bring you pleasure on a daily basis.

Former President Theodore Roosevelt once said, "Comparison is the thief of joy." I would say, "*Pain* is the thief of joy." I know because I lived it. I also know that it doesn't have to stay that way. Even if running marathons was your outlet for an adrenaline rush and a tragic accident is going to prevent you from running again, life is full of other joyous activities that can raise your heartbeat, make you smile, and provide satisfaction.

I have also learned that it is a mistake to compare suffering. Suffering is *pain without hope* in my opinion. The loss of a pinky finger to a concert pianist could be equal to the loss of a leg for a drummer.

It's not easy to accept the absence of a source of joy in your life, but moving on and finding others is possible. That is why I often say, "Suffering is everywhere; relief is *optional.*"

Let me tell you about the joy I lost from my traumatic event.

GROUNDED

Flying helicopters was a dream and a passion of mine for many years before my accident. I enjoyed it so much that when I was finally able to afford it, I hired a full-time instructor to teach me how to spread my wings and purchased an inexpensive, rebuilt used helicopter. I then designed a medical practice and life that encouraged me to fly three to five days per week.

Not only was flying a hobby that I loved, but I used it as a means of transportation to get to work a lot. After all, gridlock does not exist when you're thousands of feet above ground.

A few days after my accident, I had a flight lesson scheduled with my instructor. At this point, I knew what I was doing and my instructor was always present for safety reasons. On most lessons, he felt comfortable allowing me to perform the pre-flight inspection, assume the controls right away, get us off the ground, and land safely. On this particular day, things went a little differently.

My instructor and I met at the aircraft (parked on my back lawn), exchanged friendly greetings, and began the preflight routine to examine the helicopter. I had committed these safety protocols to memory a long time ago and had performed all the steps many times. I knew the routine like the back of my hand.

My instructor had no knowledge of my accident a few nights before. I began to look over the helicopter, acting as if nothing had happened. My acting job, however, was not sufficient to cover up the trouble I was having with the safety check.

As I began to struggle with some things that had become second nature to me by that point, I occasionally glanced toward my instructor and saw a look of concern on his face. Actually, I could *feel* his anxiety, as I was deviating from the sequences like never before.

At first, he chalked it up to me being tired or maybe stressed out from something in my personal life. He gave me the benefit of the doubt, which was comforting. However, as I continued to struggle, he made the decision to finish the preflight check on his own and later take control of the flight with me from his passenger seat for the day.

That sobering moment gave me some bitter food for thought. It was a defining moment that made me rethink my accident. "Do I need more help than I thought?" I wondered. "Am I really okay, or am I in the same state of denial that I see so many of my patients in?" As I was wondering this, my back started tensing up and hurting. If I was paying more attention, I would have realized that the pain was giving me the answer to the questions I was asking myself.

Several days later, it became clear that something from that accident had shaken up more than my back and left arm. The fatigue was constant and the pain was getting worse. My interactions with others were falling off the rails as well. I was short-tempered, bitter, and not a lot of fun to be around.

The aborted helicopter lesson provided the wake-up call I needed to eventually seek a professional diagnosis for the pain, discomfort, and other challenges I was experiencing. In that regard, I'm happy it happened. I can say that *now*; I could not and did not say that *then*.

Not long after, I saw a neurologist for a formal diagnosis of my troubles. That was when I first heard the words I was hoping to avoid—mTBI or mild traumatic brain injury. These words were describing *me*, not a patient of mine. The denial began!

I suppose that as a physician, I had an inkling of what was happening to me internally, but I was hoping it was something different—something more temporary. That was not the case, however. I was experiencing the effects of postconcussive syndrome. More specifically, I had suffered an mTBI with MCD, mild cognitive deficits.

This presented a strange role reversal for me, and I didn't like it. I had to accept that I was now the patient in the waiting room, not the doctor working in the exam room.

Mild Traumatic Brain Injuries (mTBI)

Don't let the term "mild" fool you. There is nothing mild about any brain injury. A mild traumatic brain injury is usually considered less damaging, but can still be quite severe. It can mean the MRI or CT scan or x-rays were negative for significant injury.

FINDING ACCEPTANCE

Stubbornness and denial presented a psychological barrier to acceptance of my mTBI. I needed to somehow jump that hurdle, which would allow me to prioritize self-care and begin my healing process.

Changes were needed, personally and professionally. I could continue to practice medicine, but I had to delegate more responsibility. Altering my professional role—even slightly—tore a small hole in the fabric of my sense of identity. Without acceptance, that tear opened larger.

I've never been comfortable sharing the details of my accident or how it impacted me. Admittedly, my pride was a big deterrent and, yes, denial is something just about every trauma victim must conquer.

As I write this book, there is still a bit of pride that gets in the way of me sharing my story fully, but at least I can admit that now. That would have been impossible a few years ago. Denial, however—that part of my story is gone.

My accident happened, and it changed me, more in the beginning than now, but there were a lot of adjustments to make. The biggest and most important adjustment I made was that I've learned how to not let it *control* me. I'm living a much *better* life today than I was when denial was still in play.

Most importantly to me, however, is that I am married to my best friend, the mother of all four of our children and the love of my youth and the love of my life. In fact, I married her twice. Yes, we were originally married on June 1, 1986, and then again on September 26, 2008. My accident didn't cause my divorce in 2001 but it certainly didn't help. Knowing that we came back from a bitter and protracted divorce and reunited our family is a gift that fills me with eternal gratitude.

The point is if sharing my story by writing this book helps just one person (maybe you) realize they're not alone and that *better* is possible, then sharing all of this will have been immeasurably worth the effort. *Better* likely won't mean life like it once was, but it may mean a lot more joy and a lot less pain in your life than you feel today.

If you're accustomed to living as a highly functioning adult and now find yourself struggling to juggle all of the things you used to manage with ease, you probably feel a lack of self-worth, as if you're no longer capable of caring for yourself and performing the daily tasks you once did. I put great effort into keeping those feelings private and was embarrassed to admit to any supposed weakness. That was a big mistake looking back, because it delayed my healing process for a long time.

If you find yourself in a similar situation, my advice is: *Don't be stubborn. Accept your struggles, allow people to help, delegate when necessary, and focus on healing—physically and mentally.*

Accepting my new reality took a long time for me. My world started to contract. Before my injury, I had so many balls up in the air; there was a seven location multiple-facility medical practice to run with over fifty employees and a large payroll, family commitments, parenting, social activities, and much more. My father was fighting for his life and I wanted to be there in South Florida with him and my siblings.

Now, all I really had to think about was my pain. There was so little of what I was accustomed to enjoying that I could still do. I couldn't even jump in the helicopter and take a flight to enjoy the natural beauty of our world from a higher perspective. That head-clearing joy was gone.

Subsequently, my relationships hit a point of steady deterioration, where pain, anger, frustration, and general negativity became too large a part of my personality. Still, I thought that somehow I could push through the pain. I told myself that now I just had to exert more energy to power through tasks than I had before, but everything would be fine. That stubbornness was so counterproductive.

I tried, to no avail, to rev that engine as high as I could. Every day and night, I wished my situation was something different than it was. I desperately wanted to go back to my life before the accident. I wasted a lot of energy that way.

> If you've suffered a traumatic brain injury and
> find yourself in a similar state of stubborn resis-
> tance, I feel you, but understand that you can
> only rev that engine so hot before it fails. Trying
> harder to accomplish things might seem admirable,
> but more admirable is to seek the assistance
> of others when you need it. That way, you can
> focus much more of your energy on getting better
> in the long term.

More than anything else, I needed to find acceptance. One of the first things I had to let go of was my helicopter. I loved flying, but it didn't make sense to hold onto that. Maybe someday I could get back to it, but at least for the short term, I needed to remove it from my to-do list, so I could concentrate on the more important things . . . like healing.

I finally made the painful decision to sell the helicopter and part ways with my instructor. My energy could no longer be wasted wishing for a past that was never coming back. Praying for the impossible and denying the present was not helping me.

Saying goodbye to flying provided space in my world to dedicate to things like rekindling my relationship with my children. The separation from my wife and ultimate divorce took a toll on them that I only now have begun to comprehend. I desperately wanted to "fix" my situation and family, but that would come much later. I had to heal first.

Relationships—we'll talk more about them throughout the book. They're a particularly tough challenge when pain and injury is a major part of your life. For now, just know that if your time with family and friends seems more contentious, bitter, or difficult . . . it's normal, and I've been there.

Shortly after I sold the helicopter, I decided to start being completely honest with people about my accident. Opening up in that way helped me to shift my focus from internal anger to an outward display of acceptance and transparency.

By acceptance, I don't mean that I accepted my pain and suffering as a forever condition or accepted that I might never feel any better. Rather, I mean I accepted the fact that my injury had happened and that I had to stop denying or ignoring the struggles associated with the resulting pain as I had been. It meant focusing my energy on the people around me who cared enough to help, and dedicating more time to finding solutions for healing. I could then begin to read extensively about my injury, seek world-class specialists, and open my mind to new possibilities for healing.

COMMON YET COMPLEX

Today, when I sit with patients who have suffered a brain injury or commissioned me to prepare a life care plan, I usually tell them, "I can't wear your shoes, but I've worn a pair with a similar fit. I might not understand the exact things you're going through, but I understand some of them for sure."

Many people who have suffered a TBI have been stricken with far greater consequences than what I experienced, but I know how difficult my situation felt when I was in the height of its effects. As a treating physician, empathy helps me communicate my thoughts about effective therapies, medications, and more. That empathy was there before my accident, but it's now enhanced like never before. I suggest you find a physician who exudes a similar sense of compassion. As a life care planner who has dealt with trauma on a personal level, my understanding of my clients' situation encourages and enables me to account for everything they may need throughout their lifetime.

Injuries to the brain are, unfortunately, quite common. In fact, the Centers for Disease Control and Prevention estimate that approximately 1.5 million Americans suffer a traumatic brain injury (TBI) each year.

Sadly, not only are brain injuries quite common, they're also quite complex. Some of the patients I've treated have suffered deep wounds that have penetrated their skull and caused damage that will affect their cognitive ability forever. Once brilliant businesspeople and genius innovators can become much like children in the wake of brain trauma. It's a sad but true state of affairs. Other brain injuries will result in strong personality changes, diminished mental capacity, coma, or worse. Some deteriorate and worsen over time.

Other serious consequences from TBIs include seizures, balance problems, chronic fatigue, language difficulties, impaired vision, and more. Cognitive issues are common. Psychosocial changes in mood and behavior can also lead to substance abuse, lack of impulse control, debilitating anxiety, and depression.

Life care planners need to address all of those possible TBI complications. Often, the injured party may be in a state of denial. In those situations, the life care planner must work with the family to get a clear picture of what's needed in terms of care for the injured person to move forward.

Denying Denial

Denial is a somewhat natural stage of the recovery process, especially for high achievers, who have a particularly difficult time coping with their new reality.

Acceptance does not mean you are accepting anything forever; you're merely accepting your trauma as a current obstacle you need to develop solutions for. You can't deny your way through pain and suffering. Instead, acknowledge it and move past it.

In the case of moderate to severe brain injuries, a multilayered and multispecialty approach for care is necessary. This means that several different specialists will be called upon to provide treatment, which will—no doubt—be quite expensive.

Not only is the treatment for a TBI costly, but it is also incredibly complex, involving several layers of care and rehabilitation. Additionally, there is usually a lost capacity for work involved. A comprehensive life care plan can lay out all the details regarding the complexity of TBI treatment and its associated cost.

In some cases, it's necessary to prepare two or three versions of a life care plan for the reason that different people recover differently. Therefore, the life care planner may need to account for evolving stages and rates of recovery. Flexibility, however, is a strength of the process. Life care planning has adaptability built in to account for changes in the client's condition and needs.

Despite the complexity involved, great comfort can be found in the recent advancements of the medical world in studying the human brain. One such *eureka* moment has opened the door for innovation that could prove immensely beneficial. I'm talking about the discovery of something called neuroplasticity.

NEUROPLASTICITY

Neuroplasticity refers to the brain's ability to regenerate activity in response to trauma. The medical community's understanding of this science has been growing rapidly in recent years. Studies have proved that connections in the brain will reform. This translates to enormous potential for trauma victims to relearn tasks and regain function previously thought to be forever damaged. The simple truth is that the human brain is remarkably resilient and it will fight for you.

Neuralink

Neuralink Corporation is a neurotechnology company that began in 2016. It was founded by Elon Musk and others and is headquartered in San Francisco, California. Their work with developing implantable brain–machine interfaces (BMI) has been a game changer in the healthcare industry.

At a live demonstration in August 2020, Musk described one of their early devices as "a Fitbit in your skull," which could soon cure paralysis, deafness, blindness, and other disabilities.

Diagnostic tests like functional MRIs have proven that the brain has the ability to remap itself where old connections were broken. Neuroplasticity is not a fast process, but it can be somewhat accelerated by certain therapies. If you're currently recovering from a TBI, part of your education should include learning everything you can about neuroplasticity.

The science behind neuroplasticity is important for all trauma victims, because the brain's ability to heal itself has a trickle-down effect; it can extend healing to other parts of the body. The back, neck, legs, arms, and every other system in the human body communicate with the brain. Therefore, if the brain can reconnect itself, there is hope for other injuries to jump on that pathway and also get on the fast track for healing.

Consider the story of a man named Joe Dispenza. The account of his trauma and subsequent recovery is meaningful and motivational for anyone in a similar situation. It provides verification of the brain's ability to heal itself and enable people with all kinds of injuries to get better.

As a successful chiropractic physician and running enthusiast, Joe had a great life. Career-wise, he was an esteemed professional with a large client base and history of exemplary work. Along with being an accomplished practitioner, he was also an athlete who took great pride in exercising and running competitively. He consistently participated in events—like marathons—that pushed his body to the limits. That life transformed into a completely different reality, however, on one fateful and tragic afternoon.

Joe was running a marathon one day when he was struck by an oncoming truck. For details of how the incident happened, I suggest reading one of the many inspiring books that Joe has written or attending one of his presentations in person. For our purposes, understand that the impact, as you can imagine, was catastrophic. The accident fractured *all* of the bones in Joe's spine. In the hospital, Joe was told that not only would he never run another marathon, he would also never walk again.

Heal Yourself

Joe Dispenza happily shares his story and lessons on training the human brain to heal itself through many bestselling books. I suggest any of them to help you understand what is truly possible for your own recovery, simply by having the right frame of mind.

Some of the world's best spine surgeons suggested a laminectomy as the only choice for corrective action. If you're unfamiliar, a laminectomy is a procedure that involves taking the backs of the spine off and replacing them with Harrington rods. In most cases, this is not a highly desired course of action, but surgeons told Joe that, for him, it was the *only* course of action.

As a practicing chiropractor, Joe knew a little about what the procedure involved, and he was not in love with the idea, so he elected to take his own approach. He became dedicated to learning about the mind's ability to heal the body.

Joe began to learn everything he could about neuroplasticity. He also took it a step further and began to research his understanding of God on a deeper level. The approach was a hybrid of science and spirituality that served as an accelerant for his healing process.

Eventually, Joe became so knowledgeable about neuroplasticity that he changed careers to become a neuroscientist and a best-selling author. He's the perfect example of how a tragic accident can serve as inspiration for meaningful and profound change. If you believe in silver linings, Joe Dispenza is a sterling example.

Career Change

I'll talk more about the possibility for career change in a later chapter on vocational challenges. For now, begin to consider how your trauma can be the catalyst for a new, more meaningful, satisfying, and exciting way of life.

Convinced that he could control his healing with positive energy, Joe spent most of his time lying on his stomach in a hospital bed, envisioning the appearance of a normal spine. Joe applied positive energy to seize control of his pain. He thought about what his back would look like if it were healthy. Slowly, those good thoughts translated to a physical healing of his own spine. More than just wishful thinking, Joe's spine actually realigned itself!

A surgical knife never pierced Joe's back. Yet, not only did he walk again, but he also established a regular running routine as well. Some called it a medical miracle, but that almost cheapens the reality of Joe's accomplishments. What he did was real. He had a tragic accident, couldn't walk, and used the power within his own mind to heal himself.

Sure, it's easy to cast doubt on Joe's story or proclaim his words as those of a false prophet. If that's the case, I implore you to investigate Joe's story a little deeper for yourself. Read, listen, or consume his message in any of his media forms to judge for yourself. The worst thing that could happen is that you simply don't believe what he has to say. The best thing that could happen is that you apply his teachings and heal your own trauma. When put in those terms, it seems almost foolish not to at least give it a shot. What have you got to lose?

Consider for a moment the story and work of Dr. John Ernest Sarno Jr. (June 23, 1923–June 22, 2017). Sarno was Professor of Rehabilitation Medicine, New York University of Medicine, and attending physician at the Howard A. Rusk Institute of Rehabilitation Medicine, New York University Medical Center.

He graduated from Kalamazoo College, Kalamazoo, Michigan, in 1943, and Columbia University College of Physicians and Surgeons in 1950. In 1965, he was appointed the director of the outpatient department at the Rusk Institute.

Sarno originated the term tension myositis syndrome (TMS) to name a psychosomatic condition producing pain, particularly back pain. Although rejected by his mainstream peers, the theory of TMS and Sarno's treatment of it have been hailed by many laypeople as life-changing. A 2017 book on back pain treatments described Sarno as the "rock star of the back world." A documentary on his life and work titled *All the Rage (Saved by Sarno)* was released in 2016.

I'm a licensed and trained medical doctor with hundreds of thousands of hours of clinical practice, which means I know all about the power of *real* medicine, and I believe strongly in it. However, after reading what Joe has to say and living through my own experience, I also believe strongly in the power within our mind.

Neuroplasticity can be leveraged to produce wonderful healing effects; one of those is as a coping mechanism for anxiety.

Many—if not all—TBI sufferers experience tremendous anxiety, and some deal with debilitating depression. If you're experiencing those issues, understand that they don't have to be part of your life forever.

Your brain is capable of amazing healing power. Educate yourself about neuroplasticity and the many possibilities for positive change within your own mind. This includes meditation, prayer, restorative sleep, reading books by inspirational authors like Joe Dispenza (obviously, many others exist as well), and anything else that can get you to live a better day.

The healing power within our own thoughts is immense. In a way, it involves calling upon the resiliency of our childhood. The child's mind is generally not bogged down with worry or anxiety. Rather, it accepts things for the way they are, maintains an infinite curiosity, and does not waste time thinking about what could have been.

In the next chapter, you'll learn about the remarkable spirit of a young girl who, despite being the victim of a tragic house fire, maintained a positive energy that was contagious to everyone around her. Learn how a team of professionals rallied around her cause and designed a life care plan that enabled her to get better every day.

Guided Meditation

Technology has made our lives easier in many ways.
If you're curious about beginning a meditation practice as
part of a healing process, there are several great apps on
your phone, tablet, or laptop that can help. Look into down-
loading Headspace or Calm—among others—to help you
get started. I still to this day use both of them.

Chapter 3

Burn Injuries:
Covering the Costs of Healing

*"We do not need magic to transform our world.
We carry all the power we need
inside ourselves already."*

—J.K. Rowling (author)

I received a call one night from a plaintiff attorney whom I had worked with in the past. He asked me if I would be willing to work on a life care plan for his client. I had already worked with this attorney a few times before, so I was open to the idea and asked him to provide details about the situation.

The attorney told me that his clients were the family members and legal guardians of a charming seven-year-old girl named Makela. Sadly, Makela had suffered massive burns, accounting for about 40 percent of the frontal surface area of her skin, mostly on her upper body. Significant scarring was present on her hands, arms, face, neck, and a small portion of her lower body.

Not only was Makela's appearance affected by the burns, but so were her movements. She had developed contractures in her hands and arms, which happens when the elastic skin that covers a joint is damaged and replaced with a more fibrous tissue. The result is abnormal and sometimes involuntary movement. Contractures are common symptoms of burn victims and people with cerebral palsy. As a result of this and her burns, Makela attended frequent appointments at the burn center for evaluations and grafts.

My heart broke as the attorney told me more of her story, like it often does when I hear about children who are the victims of trauma.

Makela had been living in an old rented house with her mother and older sister. It was a wooden building that needed extensive repairs, not only to the structure itself, but also to the electrical system.

Somehow, repair to the wiring in the home went awry, and a horrifying electrical fire ensued. Smoke quickly overwhelmed the home as rescue personnel rushed in to save whomever they could find.

Miraculously, firefighters emerged with a severely wounded but still breathing Makela. They were not, however, able to save the other two family members. Makela's mother and older sister succumbed to the flames and died.

When the immediate repercussions of the tragedy began to settle, Makela was left in the care of her uncle and grandparent, who served as legal guardians. Their family attorney immediately recognized the need to have a life care plan drawn up as soon as possible to ensure Makela would get the level of care she needed.

When I met with Makela in her family attorney's office, she was still at the beginning of her recovery. I've discovered that when working with children, it's particularly important to establish a relationship based on trust and friendship. So, I didn't want to approach her wearing a lab coat and using medical terminology that would scare her or make her uncomfortable. I was fortunate that the family attorney could also vouch for my trustworthiness and approachability.

As it turns out, Makela was such a friendly, free spirit, she would have welcomed me with open arms no matter how I dressed or what I said. She opened up to me almost immediately.

I quickly noticed that Makela had no fear talking to anyone. She easily walked up to other children and adults and engaged effortlessly in heart-to-heart conversations, as if she had known them for her entire life. What's more impressive is that she did this in spite of her altered physical appearance. She had no reservations about the way she looked in the eyes of others. To me, that was as inspiring as anything I had ever seen before. Makela was one of the most special little girls I have ever had the pleasure of knowing.

Makela's innocence and good-natured personality were like a magic elixir for the surviving family members, who were understandably grief-stricken about their losses. They were mourning the death of Makela's mother and sister, but one interaction with Makela was always enough to bring a smile to their face.

I was more determined than ever to write an undeniably accurate, credible, and comprehensive life care plan for Makela, because she made such a positive impression on me. I made it my personal mission to ensure she would receive all the services she would need, not just presently, but for the rest of her life.

As a rehabilitation physician, I had already worked with many burn patients, but never as a life care planner. Because of that, I decided to coauthor the document with another, more experienced life care planner. I was only about three years into my new career as a physician life care planner at that point, and wanted to be sure none of Makela's needs went unaccounted for; no treatment, device, specialist, or anything else related to her care could be left out.

The second time I met with Makela was at the Shriners Hospital in Tampa, which was also the location for the rest of our visits. There I met and developed an effective rapport with her doctors. We discussed and elaborated upon the layers of care that would be involved for Makela going forward.

Makela's life care plan was going to need to cover a comprehensive list of coordinated therapies, procedures, and appointments. At first glance, extensive treatment to manage the pain and appearance of her burns was critical. Beyond that, however, was the need for access to excellent psychological treatment if she needed it as she got older.

Despite her resilience, Makela had already suffered from post-traumatic stress disorder (PTSD). Therefore, a psychiatrist was brought in to reassure Makela that she wasn't going to be pulled from a burning building every time she went to bed at night.

Makela was doing beyond an admirable job of coping with the loss of her mother and sister. Much of that may have had to do with the remarkable resilience of childhood. However, the emergence of additional psychological issues was also a possibility at any given moment of her young life.

As she grew up, Makela was certain to be challenged with the absence of those family members as integral parts of her life. Without a doubt, adolescence and early adulthood were also going to present tremendous difficulties as Makela tried to fit in with her peers. It's hard enough for most young people to feel comfortable in their own skin; imagine what that's like when almost half of your skin is disfigured.

TREATMENT

As a medical student, and resident physician, I spent considerable time training and working in a burn unit, and quickly realized that it's a role that can only be fulfilled by special individuals. Unfortunately, treatment for burns usually involves a painful process in and of itself. Therefore, only those who can express sincere empathy are cut out for such a role. They also need to see the pathway of inflicting temporary pain on the patient to provide long-term benefit. Furthermore, they need to have an effective way of communicating with the patient that the discomfort of the treatment is worth the healing it provides.

Burns are often cited as the greatest pain a human being can endure due to the massive number of nerve endings contained in our skin. Placing a young child into a situation like that seems unfathomable. Because the skin is so sensitive and the largest organ in our body, treatment for burns presents many challenges.

There is no quick fix for burns. Some injuries can be addressed with one surgery, treatment, or procedure. With burns, however, certain areas heal faster than others and, in many situations, therapy must continue for several years.

Care providers usually need to administer powerful pain medication just to remove the bandages and apply clean dressings. They also need to peel off the dead, burnt skin to provide a healthy vascular bed where new skin can grow or a graft can be applied.

The most painful time for a burn victim is usually in the beginning. After a while, the pain generally dissipates to a much more tolerable level when given sufficient time to heal. Regular dressing changes, compression garments, and physical therapy help a lot. Most often, there will be some form of neuropathic pain that remains, but the initial trauma will assuage over time and with proper medical attention.

THE BENEFITS OF LIFE CARE PLANNING ASAP

One of the unique complications in assembling Makela's life care plan was that her arms had sustained extremely severe burns. The family didn't have the financial resources or required insurance coverage to pay for the treatment to repair that damage. Therefore, we had to find a team of people, including a supremely skilled occupational therapist, who could treat her while litigation was pending. Life care planning could not wait in this situation; it had to begin immediately.

Getting treatment before a case is settled is often an early hurdle for trauma victims. The funds may not be immediately available to pay for costly, but necessary, treatments. Attorneys should always be aware of how beneficial it is to secure a life care planner early in the process, without waiting for a settlement and dealing with the risks and expenses of a trial.

If you're in a similar situation to Makela's family, where you need treatment during a pending litigation case, but lack sufficient funds or coverage to make it happen, having a CPLC and an attorney with an exemplary reputation working for you can be an invaluable resource to help get you the care you need.

Because I was brought into Makela's life care planning early, I was able to start thinking about the endgame for her care right away. I started thinking about how I could leverage my relationships with a community of providers. This is undoubtedly a distinct advantage to having a physician acting as your life care planner.

The family's attorney was also excellent at making things happen for Makela. He spared no expense in his pursuit of determining the liability side of the case and getting her family the maximum amount of damages.

Her attorney, a community of providers, and I banded together to get this amazing child the care she needed through what's called a *letter of protection*. This is a legally binding document that states all care providers will forgo any collections efforts while the client's case is pending. It's basically a medical IOU.

If Makela's family had to go through Medicaid or some other form of assistance, she would have never received the expert level of care she got via the letter of protection. Medicaid is especially limited in the treatments it will pay for.

COORDINATED CARE

As part of Makela's team, we enlisted the services of several qualified professionals. Our first assignment was a case manager. We couldn't expect Makela's uncle or grandparent to coordinate the massive entanglement of red tape involved with medical care, so we brought this case manager in to work strictly on coordinating outpatient visits, transportation arrangements, doctor appointments, medication, therapists, and more.

The case manager served an especially important role in Makela's situation, because the family had enough to deal with already, making sure her basic needs for food, shelter, and clothing were met. Plus, they had to do it all while grieving the loss of two beloved family members.

Case Management

Even when a child still has the love and care of both parents available, the coordination of all these providers can be time-consuming. Case management becomes almost impossible in a home with two working parents who have other children to consider as well.

Several other team members were dedicated to Makela's case, as well. For instance, a vocational specialist performed an evaluation to investigate and determine how her injuries would affect her future earning capacity. This assessment played a big role in figuring out the total dollar amount of damages requested in her life care plan.

Furthermore, an economist was enlisted to determine the effects of inflation on the services Makela would need as she grew older. Therapists were brought in to secure the best compression garments for Makela's physical therapy to alleviate her contractures.

ENSURING MAKELA'S FUTURE

Makela's case is a good example of the importance of having the right team behind you to raise your level of care. Her attorney had an outstanding relationship with the community, which went a long way in getting people to help her. My experience as a medical provider also helped, because I was able to reach out to colleagues who were willing to get involved in this special case.

As a life care planner, it's a wonderful feeling to play an integral part of such a worthy cause. The care team we assembled was composed of special people who genuinely wanted to do the right thing. Together, we overcame the barriers that insufficient funds and lack of insurance coverage put up. It was proof positive of the power of people working together.

We had secured the testimony of treating physicians and I was confident that the plan my colleague and I created was bulletproof. The foundation of Makela's life care plan was unquestionable, and there were no missing pieces to the level of care she would receive from it.

Everyone on the plaintiff's side was ready to go to trial. The attorney had everyone well prepared. On the night before the scheduled court date, however, the two sides came to a settlement, which is where the vast majority of these cases are resolved.

At the end of the settlement, Makela's family and care team were confident that she had the best possible outcome for her litigation. Her attorney arranged to have a special needs trust established to ensure the money recovered would be there for the rest of her life.

Today, Makela is about twelve years old. Despite the injuries she suffered and the permanent losses she endured, she hasn't gone through any major bouts of depression and is doing remarkably well in school. Her attorney and I have always had a good working relationship, so he occasionally updates me on her progress. Most importantly, he tells me that her indomitable spirit continues to shine.

Physicians, attorneys, life care planners, and others are willing to lend a hand when needed. If you find yourself in a situation where you're struggling to handle the cost of medically necessary treatments, ask your doctor, lawyer, life care planner, therapist, or another professional who might have a strong presence of goodwill in their community. They might be able to assemble something for you similar to the way we were able to coordinate great care for Makela.

Forever Losses

There are certain damages accounted for in life care plans that are incalculable and forever. In Makela's case, she lost her mother and sister and there is no way to place a dollar figure on such a loss. We can, however, ensure that every aspect of her education, lost earning capacity, and any associated psychological treatments are provided.

The loss of family members and the suffering it causes are called noneconomic damages because our economic system provides no easily accessible associated value for them. The only funds that can be assigned to such a loss fall under the category of pain and suffering, which can be included in the legal proceedings, but not accounted for in the life care plan.

Makela's case exemplifies not only the power of healing found within a child's positive attitude, but also the benefits of having a care team with a unified goal. In the next chapter, I'll discuss how a care team can accomplish amazing things for a trauma victim that extends from day one of a young life, all the way through adulthood.

Chapter 4

Birth Injuries: Living Proof of the Unstoppable Human Spirit

"Everything you want is on the other side of fear."

—Jack Canfield (author)

Many years ago, an attorney friend of mine introduced me to a woman named Eileen from South Florida. Eileen had given birth to triplets; one did not survive birth and the other two were severely impaired with cerebral palsy. She needed a rehabilitation physician for the two survivors who had many physical challenges to overcome.

At an age when most children were scampering across the floor on their hands and knees, Eileen's kids were only capable of *commando crawling,* which is what happens when children don't have the strength to push themselves up when trying to move forward. Instead, they drag themselves with their arms while their stomachs lay flat on the ground.

Eileen was a protective parent who would stalk the ends of the earth to find the best possible treatments for her children.

Eventually, Eileen discovered a specialized physical therapy that could accelerate her children's progress. She found a center in Michigan that was doing amazing things for kids suffering from all types of hypoxic-ischemic encephalopathy (HIE), which is brain damage that results from a lack of oxygen supplied to a child's brain during birth. Approximately one in ten cases of HIE causes cerebral palsy.

Many times, HIE leads to cognitive impairments as well as physical difficulties. Psychosocial issues can develop as well. Some children with particularly severe brain damage will require around-the-clock care, which can place a tremendous amount of anguish and stress on family members who act as main caretakers.

The center in Michigan was using a device called the TheraSuit, which is a wearable item that positions the child in such a way that therapists can maximize muscular development. Rather than the child being floppy or on the floor, one therapist can hold the child upright, while the other works with a chosen limb. The garment has bungee cord attachments that suspend the child in a plastic-coated metal cage approximately ten feet deep by ten feet wide and six or seven feet high.

By virtue of the bungee cords, a child who has never stood on their own can be positioned slightly above the floor while bending at the knees and bouncing, which allows them to touch the floor on and off. Almost without fail, an ear-to-ear smile spreads across a child's face when they witness the upright world around them for the first time.

A thirty-day round of therapy helped Eileen's children to accomplish things that would have taken them several months or years to accomplish with traditional therapy. Finances, however, were a problem for the family, so Eileen had to work hard and save money for more treatment.

By the time she saved enough, the center had gone out of business because the owner didn't have the money to properly staff and operate it from her home location in California nearly three thousand miles away.

Persistent in her efforts to continue the treatment her children needed, Eileen tracked down the former owner of that center to a residence in California. She called her to find out if there was any possibility that the center would reopen. When the owner told her that she could no longer afford to run the business, Eileen unabashedly replied, "Then, let me buy it from you."

The owner was receptive to the idea of selling the business to Eileen. Still, Eileen had no idea how to run a business, no experience with rehabilitation, and zero knowledge of how to use the equipment. Nonetheless, she carried through on her promise to buy all of the assets and the lease.

At that point, Eileen realized she needed trained professionals to help her serve clients, so she asked me point-blank, "I'm buying the therapy center that my kids were attending, and I want to use the TheraSuit, not only for them, but to help other families as well. Will you be the center's medical director?"

It was hard to say no to Eileen. She was so determined to do the right thing for her kids and everyone else that she made me and others want to be part of a special situation. So, I agreed to join Eileen in her business venture. Together, with an attorney who introduced us, we co-founded a center called Therapies for Kids.

It didn't take long before the center became world-renowned for helping children suffering from birth injuries. While I no longer have a financial or vested interest in the center, I'm happy to say that it is still thriving today. If you find yourself with a child in need of such a service, I recommend you contact them immediately.

That center is what led me to cross paths with the two remarkable inventors of the TheraSuit—Richard and Izabella Koscielny.

Richard and Izabella were physical therapists, living and working in Poland when their daughter Kaya was born with cerebral palsy. Much like my friend Eileen, the Koscielnys were determined and they made a promise that their daughter would not have anything less than the best care possible.

The Koscielnys' invention is a miracle of innovation created by two special people who were determined to do right by their daughter and, in turn, helped other children around the world. To this day, Richard and Izabella remain two of the most amazing people I've ever had the pleasure of knowing and working with. Their daughter, Kaya, who inspired their innovation, is now a successful young adult who helps children and adults overcome their disabilities. She has grown to become an incredible advocate for special needs individuals all over the world, speaking publicly at schools and anywhere else she can get her positive message out in the open.

The Importance of Parental Mental Health

Parents want everything for their children. It can be extremely difficult for them to see their kids struggling. This can cause family members to need regularly scheduled psychological assistance of their own. This service should not be ignored in the life care plan.

Until the invention of the TheraSuit, the common belief was that twenty to sixty minutes of therapy was the maximum these children could tolerate.

Thanks to the tireless efforts of Izabella and Richard Koscielny, kids could now benefit from three to four hours per day of therapy. This model was termed *intensive* physical therapy. Essentially, it allowed kids to receive seven to eight months' worth of therapy in a thirty-day time span, which proved to make a substantial advance in their development.

This led Therapies for Kids to formulate the BiFulco Method, which implements nutritional and psychological therapies into their intensive physical therapy to produce a holistic method for the optimal treatment of children with birth injuries.

Today, various models of intensive physical therapy for children with birth injuries are much more widely accepted as an industry standard, and most insurance companies have been convinced to cover them.

Because kids grow and develop so fast—unlike adults—reevaluations need to be written into the life care plan of someone with a birth injury. Advances in technology, like the TheraSuit, are constantly being introduced, as well as innovative therapies and procedures, which creates a need to periodically reevaluate a young person's life care plan.

GETTING ANSWERS

Little did I know that my experience at Therapies for Kids would set the stage for me to become a life care planner. Years later, it was my work there that introduced me to a man named Richard Neubauer—the world's leading authority on the hyperbaric option to treat children with brain injuries and birth defects.

My interactions with Richard helped me understand the magnitude of what's needed to help kids with birth injuries. I began to understand the massive benefit kids could receive from the right therapy, treatment, and devices. Not only that, but I also came to understand the scope of the financial burden to parents and how necessary it was to account for these costs to be covered.

Life care plans that concern birth injuries usually have the highest total value attached to them because they cover the span of an entire lifetime. Many of the disabilities that come from a birth injury carry on throughout adulthood, and the plan must be written to account for all of it.

Many children who suffer from birth injuries will require attendant care for their lifetime. Some will be able to attend public school, but others will require specialized education. Most often, adaptive equipment such as handrails, ramps, walk-in showers, and other accommodations must be made to the child's home.

All of the in-home adaptive equipment, educational resources, and medical costs must be written into the life care plan. Specific medical procedures will also be anticipated at certain stages of growth, as well as occupational, physical, and speech therapies. Respite care must be provided for the parents, as well as lost wages to account for when they must tend to their children's needs and are unable to work.

Much like the situation with Makela's guardians in the previous chapter, parents of children with birth defects also need help with case management. Balancing their careers, homes, other childcare, and managing their own mental health, all while caring for a child with a birth defect, can overwhelm even the strongest of paternal figures. Doctor visits, therapy appointments, and a wide range of other necessities also need to be coordinated to optimize care.

When it comes to caring for a child with birth injuries, parents are usually struggling to come up with answers to so many big questions. *How am I going to pay for all this care? Am I still going to be able to pay the mortgage? Will I be able to put enough food on the table for the rest of my family? Do I have enough money for heat, electricity, and clothing for everybody? What about tomorrow?*

THE WARRIOR-PARENT EMERGES

Despair and frustration is often easy to see on the faces of parents who find themselves in this type of situation, but the resilience, determination, and love in their child's eyes usually gets them to reach a little deeper inside themselves and discover the warrior-parent within them.

Sometimes both parents rally around each other and their child to accomplish amazing things. Sadly, in other cases, the parents' relationship can dissolve. Occasionally, one parent emerges as the warrior, and that parent could be either the mother or the father.

If you are the parent of a child with a birth injury, a life care plan can provide answers. It can map those coordinated activities, assist a case manager, and give you the peace of mind of knowing the costs for care will be covered. As the first step out of the darkness for your child's birth injuries, seek the help of a qualified life care planner and let the document they create guide you to better days ahead.

The life care planning process brings families with similar experiences together. By working through the process, you'll engage with other parents who have already settled cases. You'll meet other families who have been through the process of raising money for their children's care. Sometimes, it helps to know that others have been there; it's comforting, as well as educational and purposeful.

Families who share these experiences often find camaraderie in each other. On any given day, they can find themselves in the role of either the motivator or the people in need of encouragement.

> Relationships with other parents who have disabled or "special needs" children can be wonderfully beneficial, but kids have it a bit harder. Most kids spend a lot of time in school, and that can be a tough experience for a child if they're the only one who looks, walks, or acts differently because of a birth defect. That's why it's important to find a school equipped to welcome a building full of

kids with physical problems or to engage them in
regular social situations with other kids who have
impairments.

A major adjustment needs to be made for parents who have
children with disabilities. They need to come to grips with the
lifetime of therapy and services their children will need. The life
care plan, along with medical advances and excellent providers,
can help them make that adjustment.

Many parents need to reach the bottom before they can rise to
the occasion. They hit a point of despair and disbelief that the
hopes they had for their child are gone. There comes a point,
however, when they realize that nobody else is more qualified
than they are to be the head coach and cheerleader for their
child to conquer their unique challenges. The warrior emerges
within parents, and it's an amazing thing to see that changeover
take place. The life care plan can help parents come to terms
with their circumstances because it provides a roadmap for how
their child can have a high quality of life, while also eliminating
any worry of financial burden.

Of course, not all parents make that adjustment to warrior sta-
tus. Sometimes, marriages don't survive. Not everyone is cut out
to be so strong and to advocate for their child in every possible
way to create the best life for them.

Siblings are also affected by having a brother or a sister with disabilities. Most often, siblings see the challenges their brother or sister is struggling through and become infinitely more compassionate and grateful for everything they have. Birth injuries affect everyone in the family in their own unique way. In most cases, parents emerge as warriors, siblings become supportive confidants, and the child with birth injuries becomes the rallying point for everyone to focus their best selves on.

Kids: Masters of the Moment

Kids are masters of the moment. They're never thinking about "what if?" To many of them, disabilities are just life. It's all they've ever known, so they don't waste time with self-pity or despair. They've got too much to do and explore to be focused on their challenges.

Magic happens when a child with disabilities arrives at a therapy center and works with a therapist who "gets it," one who understands the infinite curiosity, dogged determination, and remarkable resilience of kids—with or without disabilities.

All you have to do is spend ten minutes with a child who is challenged with a disability to understand that they want to grow up and do all the things that other kids do. And that they can. It might just look a little bit different.

Chapter 5

Multitrauma:
Healing Against All Odds

*"I love that this morning's sunrise
does not define itself by
last night's sunset."*

—Steve Maraboli (author)

I'll never forget the evening of January 25, 1990. Amid the cold and snowy darkness in East Meadow, New York, that night, I was in the process of completing my residency at the Nassau County Medical Center.

As a fourth-year resident, I was used to being called into work in the emergency room on any given day or night. Many times, there were too many trauma victims for the staff on hand to attend to, so residents, like myself, were asked to assist.

By that point, I had seen many horrible accidents involving injuries to multiple parts of the body—the head, neck, back, legs, skin, and sometimes all of the above. Still, nothing could have prepared me for the multitude of tragic situations I witnessed on that night. I got the call late that night to get to the emergency room as soon as possible. The news was chilling. Avianca Airlines Flight 52 from Bogota, Colombia, to New York missed the runway and crashed into the hillside of a Long Island neighborhood.

The result was seventy-three fatalities (including eight of the nine crew members) and eighty-five injuries, many of whom were heading to Nassau County with multitrauma. Evidently, the plane ran out of fuel, but it was really a *series* of ill-timed and miscommunicated events that ultimately caused the crash.

Basically, everything that could have gone wrong did. Bad weather, fuel miscalculations, and misunderstandings between the crew and air traffic control at JFK International Airport—where the plane was trying to land—were all contributing factors.

As I walked through the tunnels that connected the residents' living quarters to the main campus that night, I tried to prepare myself for the chaos I had been told to expect. With a steady onslaught of people needing immediate attention, the hospital staff was doing its best to control the situation. My role was mostly to assist in the triage, which meant I assessed the incoming patients, pointed people in the right direction, and implemented life-sustaining treatment when necessary.

I saw so many people managing through incredible pain and suffering. Some had sepsis that needed to be treated; others had gastrointestinal damage that required a colostomy bag until their colon could be repaired. The worst of the victims were in such danger that they needed a ventilator while life-saving procedures were executed.

Because Nassau County was a Level I trauma center and located just a few miles away from the crash site, we received a large number of the victims. It was all-hands-on-deck and time was of the essence for people with multiple fractures, vascular injuries, amputation, severe burns, multiorgan system failure, and more. I don't know exactly how many people we treated, but most of them endured a recovery process that lasted weeks, months, years, or their entire lives.

Eventually, I saw survivors make their journey from on-the-spot life-saving procedures to walking out of the hospital under their own power. That experience spoke to me about not only the power of advanced medical treatment, but the possibilities that exist when skilled professionals come together.

The long-term effects of that night on me were interesting. In one way, it prepared me—as a rehabilitation physician—to handle almost any multitrauma situation imaginable. At the time, however, I didn't realize how well that experience would equip me to be a life care planner as well.

Life care planning is at its best when people of various disciplines communicate about how to provide optimal care for patients in their greatest time of need, and that's exactly what happened that night at Nassau County Medical Center.

LIFE CARE PLANNING FOR MULTITRAUMA

A life care plan for someone with multitrauma usually involves a wide spectrum of medical providers. Trauma surgeons, orthopedists, vascular specialists, neurologists, therapists, and others could all be involved.

Having a future state in mind is particularly important in this type of scenario. You don't need to think so far ahead that it overwhelms you, but you want to know what milestones lie ahead, so that you can at least gauge your progress.

If doubt creeps into your mind about a treatment or procedure, ask questions. The next time your doctors chat by your bedside during their morning or evening rounds, pay careful attention. Be *infinitely curious* about your situation.

By becoming an active participant in your treatment, you'll be able to identify the people on your team who have the most compassion and will communicate clearly and specifically about an appropriate vision of the future. Find that individual or group of individuals who can help you shift focus from pain and suffering to the better days ahead.

When your life care planner is also a physician, they'll be able to identify your multitrauma needs quickly and develop a plan for your healing. From there, a CPLCP will enlist the right specialists for your specific injuries as soon as possible.

> If an injury to the spinal cord has occurred, you need people who are especially aware of injuries to the senses. Early on, someone needs to check for problems with loss of balance, hearing, sight, smell, touch, and taste. If any of these are present, the appropriate rehabilitation procedures should begin immediately.

Physician life care planners are usually supported by a community of specialists and providers, which makes communication among your care team much more fluid. They're accustomed to talking the talk (a.k.a. speaking medical language), so they can communicate with neurosurgeons, orthopedists, neurologists, endocrinologists, ophthalmologists, urologists, gastrointestinal specialists, and others fluently. Then, they can help you to better understand the roadmap for your recovery, and all of the different elements and intricacies it entails.

THE PRELIMINARY LIFE CARE PLAN

In many multitrauma cases, an attorney or close family member of the patient may reach out to a life care planner early in the process. It can be helpful in that situation if the planner can, at the outset, assemble the puzzle of what's likely to come. This way, all interested parties—including the defense attorney and their clients, and often insurance companies—will have knowledge of the framework involved.

When a life care planner is brought in early enough, they might create a *preliminary* life care plan that enables the injured party and their family to quickly focus on the future. The attorney also gains a credible resource to get oriented with the dollar figure that should be associated with the person's injuries.

A preliminary life care plan is a lot like getting an estimate from a contractor on a kitchen remodel. In that case, the person walks into your existing kitchen, looks around, takes some notes and measurements, asks questions about what you want, and then provides an estimate.

In the case of a multitrauma accident, the life care planner will talk to the patient and care team members, get an idea of the patient's current state, and write up a description of the diagnostic tests, specialists, therapists, devices, and procedures that are necessary. Then, they can provide an estimate of the associated costs to request during litigation.

If you're a victim of multitrauma, a life care plan will help you to see the financial resources you'll need and are entitled to receive. More importantly, you'll start to see the roadmap for your recovery in an organized list of phases and associated milestones. Part II of this book will take that roadmap a step further, as we begin to discuss more about your posttrauma life.

In the moments, days, and weeks following your incident, a lot gets thrown at you: a potentially lengthy hospital stay; follow-up appointments with doctors, therapists, and others; visits with your lawyer to plan your upcoming litigation; and more. It's a whirlwind of activity that you never asked for. Pause now, take a deep breath, and through meditation, or prayer, or another form of mental or emotional healing, seek peace. Ask yourself during this difficult time, what is my source of strength or hope? If you don't have one, consider seeking one now.

Once that onslaught of an uncomfortable and complicated to-do list begins to calm down, you'll need to refocus your energies on your posttrauma life. First up is understanding pain better. With that understanding comes better management and at least some sense of physical relief from it.

You'll also need to think about your new lifestyle and a career moving forward, as well as what to expect from your litigation case. By this book's final pages, you will have a deeper understanding of your trauma and how a life care plan isn't just a tool used for litigation, but also something that can assist you throughout your lifetime.

PART II

Your Posttrauma Roadmap

Chapter 6

Managing Pain: Getting from *"Why Me?"* to *"Thank You"*

"Do not resist the pain. Allow it to be there. Surrender to the grief, despair, fear, loneliness, or whatever form the suffering takes. Witness it without labeling it mentally. Embrace it. Then see how the miracle of surrender transmutes deep suffering into deep peace. This is your crucifixion. Let it become your resurrection and ascension."

—Eckhart Tolle (author)

"Why me?" I wondered every time that pain started as a dull ache in the middle of my back and continued to bang around like a steel drum lodged in my chest. Soon enough, the feeling would amplify enough to create the equivalent of a five-piece rock band of pain all over my back, chest, arms, and head.

I sometimes wondered, "If there is such a thing as God, why would he do this to me?" I knew better. I had been raised to know that God exists, but I still asked the question. We all either have "the God of our understanding, or we don't." That doesn't change the truth, only the truth we know.

Questioning one's faith or place in the universe is a normal reaction to a traumatic event. In fact, it proves that your mind is trying to find answers, which is a positive sign in your recovery.

Chronic pain usually starts in one area of the body, affects an adjacent joint, and spreads like a metastatic cancer from there. For instance, if you have thoracic pain—like I had—it's likely to affect your cervical and lumbar areas as well. Likewise, if you have knee pain, it's probably going to impact your ankle and hip. I've learned that pain is not complacent; it's an explorer. Pain wants to travel to as many destinations in your body as you will allow.

My pain began in the waking hours of the morning and escalated throughout the day. By lunchtime, it felt like a hot knife cutting through the middle of my back and slightly off to the left side, almost as if it were slicing a loaf of bread at an angle. When the pain got to that level, it became difficult to listen or engage in any conversation.

A big part of my problem in managing my pain was my refusal to respect its presence. It was controlling me because I wouldn't pay attention to it. I needed to reverse that power of control. But how?

My pain traveled to my left arm and gave me a tingling sensation, like I was hitting my funny bone all day long without ceasing. Eventually, it started to burn. At the apex of intensity, my pain reached the base of my skull, which resulted in intolerable headaches.

Eventually, I underwent a surgical procedure to free up the nerve in my elbow, which alleviated the numbness and burning there. That wasn't a horrible experience at all; I was given a local block and was put into a "twilight sleep" with the magic of anesthesia.

My thoracic spine pain was another story altogether. The very thought of burning my nerves through an injection where the needle tip is heated to 140 degrees Fahrenheit, a procedure called radiofrequency ablation (RFA), or radiofrequency neu-rotomies, was frightening. I mean, let's be honest: I referred others for such procedures, but this was *me*. The fear and appre-hension might have been more unpleasant than the actual pain, and the discomfort of the RFA was short-lived. In fact, I barely felt anything at all during the procedure, again thanks to the magic of anesthesia and a great pain management physician, Dr. Chevis James.

Radiofrequency Ablation (RFA)

RFA is a procedure that uses an electrode connected to a needle, which is inserted into the affected area. Once the needle is in place, the electrode is heated in an attempt to burn the sensory nerves away and make the pain stop.

The worst part about the RFA procedure is that it's semiperma-nent, meaning it can provide a somewhat long-lasting benefit but the relief does not last forever. Sure, it ablates (or destroys) the nerves, which eliminates the pain signals being sent to the brain. However, the human body is resilient—and not always in a favorable way. Those nerves slowly regenerate and so does the pain.

EMERGING FROM THE DARKNESS

The physical pain I experienced was only the beginning; just as real was the emotional pain. As I've discussed (and you might relate to), my pain was so disruptive that it *stole my joy*. I smiled easily before my injury, but not afterward. For most of my life, anyone who knew me would have described me as gregarious, optimistic, and a lover of life. My dear mother, Lena, would introduce me as "her happy son," one of six siblings. Postinjury, bitterness and anger overwhelmed my zest for anything.

Although a touch of depression crept in and out of my mind, I never tried to take my own life. I thought about it many times, but never seriously. *Attempting* suicide and *thinking about it* are vastly different mindsets. So if you are reading this and can relate, take a deep breath.

Thinking about suicide is sadly somewhat common among people who have suffered trauma. Posttrauma thoughts like that might even be part of the normal processing of your injury. Your life changes so much, and you must think about how to get over the obstacles you need to move forward.

If you start to put an actual plan in place to follow through on those thoughts, that's when you should reach out for help. Find a confidant to share your thoughts with. If you're too fearful or ashamed to talk to a close friend or family member about them, find a trusted psychologist, physician, healthcare worker, or even an attorney. Tell them how the pain—both emotional and physical—is affecting your state of mind.

When you talk through these thoughts with someone else, they will be able to provide you with at least *one* reason why you shouldn't do it. One reason is enough, but throughout the course of the conversation, you may realize *several* reasons why you shouldn't seriously consider taking your own life.

Be particularly aware if you have suicidal thoughts while taking prescription narcotics. One benzodiazepine and a glass of wine could cause you to never wake up again. Law enforcement calls those instances "accidental suicide." It doesn't take much when narcotics are involved, so please be careful.

I was able to extinguish any thoughts I had about suicide by considering the mess I would leave behind for my children, Dominic, Angelina, and Santo. I had already forced them to endure some mistakes I made as a husband and a father in the past. How could I possibly be so selfish to make them deal with this additional burden?

My kids became my primary reason to get better, but I found a secondary cause within my own DNA. A big part of my personal makeup was to never be a quitter.

Medical school was tough, parenting wasn't easy, and operating a medical practice was challenging. But I never gave up on any of those things. "Why," I figured, "would I give up now because one impaired driver crashed into my vehicle?"

Suicide, I decided, was the answer to *nothing*. Call it an escape if you want, but it seemed more like quitting to me. I was not about to let one incident determine the outcome of my life. I had worked far too hard to allow that to happen. Instead, I was going to do everything within my power to create and shape my vision of the future.

I knew I had the ability to be a good father, so I realized that I needed to get my act together. I had to repair the damage I had done to my marriage and reconcile with my wife—the wonderful mother of my children. I needed to convert my thinking from "Why me?" to something more positive, useful, and motivating.

THE INTERCONNECTEDNESS OF BODY, MIND, AND SPIRIT

To find a more positive mindset, explore the interconnectedness of your physical body, your feelings, and your spiritual awareness.

Fatigue, anxiety, sleep disturbances, guilt, hopelessness, and depression can all creep into your mind when pain dominates your body. Relationships can become contentious and social activities can transform from an enjoyable experience to an unwelcome obligation. In fact, pain can cause you to avoid all of the things you used to love.

Suddenly, things like playing golf, tennis, or even just cards lose their luster, sharing dinner with friends becomes a chore, and simple conversation with family and friends seems more bothersome and annoying than beneficial or enjoyable.

The problem with a lot of those activities is that pain interferes. If you're at a birthday party for a young niece or nephew and everyone is having a good time watching them open presents, it's hard for you to take part in the fun because the whole time you're getting a stabbing pain somewhere, or you're depressed, or both. Rather than shouting "happy birthday," all you can think of is "Why me?" over and over again.

Don't let pain continue to control you like this. Take your life back. Move past "Why me?" and get to a better quality of life by addressing the health of your body, mind, and spirit. This can be a gradual process, but you can get through it.

Psychological problems can be more severe when brain injuries are involved. In those cases, self-regulation and mood stability could require additional attention. Friends and family should be especially cognizant of this possibility and be ready to find help when needed.

There is no weakness in admitting to pondering this question or any other negative emotions you might be experiencing. In fact, much like physical pain, the more quickly you accept them, the faster you can heal.

Chances are, your routine has been disrupted and the life you've been accustomed to no longer exists. Your relationships could be experiencing more tension than ever before, and your social activities could have been altered, diminished, or eliminated completely. Those are difficult changes to confront.

Life care plans should be written not only with physical health at the forefront, but also psychological well-being. In fact, a significant and long-term role exists for a skilled psychologist to be written into many of them.

If pharmaceutical intervention is part of the recommended healing process, a psychiatrist may also be needed. There is no guilt, shame, or weakness in tapping into the knowledge of someone like that when trauma is involved. When working with a life care planner, be sure that the need for these professionals is fully explored and accounted for when necessary.

Psychological Help for Family Members

Trauma-induced psychological problems can extend to family members and good friends, as well. It could be equally important for those closest to you to seek counseling so they can understand what you're going through, how to best support you, and how they can process the changes in your relationship for their own benefit.

I decided to learn everything I could about my injury and my pain. By having intentional and infinite curiosity, you can give momentum to your healing process. Become inquisitive about where your pain comes from, what its effects are, and how to best manage it. Start reading everything you can about your injury. Besides books, podcasts, audiobooks, and online videos can also be helpful. A wealth of information exists about almost every case of trauma I've encountered. All you need to do is a quick online search and select the media form you prefer most.

Of all the research I did, one book helped me the most. Surprisingly, for me, it was the Bible. My younger brother, Phil, the youngest of six, was perhaps the most influential in this decision.

I was raised as a Catholic/Christian, sort of. Let me explain. As I stated previously, I was one of six siblings. I remember as a child being dropped off for church with my other siblings but never attended with my parents. So I thought, at a young age, *That's weird*. My parents did their best to instill Catholic/Christian values in all of us, but it was not until many years later that my parents had a real relationship with the God of their understanding.

The truth is, as time passed, I became less involved with church and didn't pay much attention to my faith or the God of my understanding. It's no excuse, but life got busy. I worked a lot of hours, had a family to raise, and many other commitments that consumed what seemed like twenty-five hours per day. My injury slowed all of that down, however.

I delegated many of my responsibilities at work. My family time, unfortunately, became challenging mostly because I was so difficult to deal with. All of a sudden, my to-do list shrank to almost nothing. At that point, I had all the time in the world to rediscover my faith—another sterling example of a silver lining from a situation that—on the surface—seemed like nothing but darkness.

I wanted to find out what the Bible could teach me about pain. If I was going to get an answer about God's plan for me, I figured this was the resource that would give it to me. Although the Bible didn't provide a verse that spelled out the meaning of pain for me, or tell me why this awful thing happened, it pointed me in the right direction.

The word "pain" or some form of it appears over seventy times in scripture. I believe each person must find for themselves what scripture means when it speaks of pain. Perhaps, most importantly, the Bible did explain the all-important concept of *forgiveness*.

A Spiritual Disclaimer

My spiritual journey is not meant to persuade you to any specific religion or faith. I believe each person must find the "God of their own understanding." I mention it merely because it helped me to achieve a healthier emotional state, and if it can do the same for you, I want to make sure you know about it. Explore whatever belief you have in the universe, life, nature, or God to come to a similar peace.

If faith isn't in your repertoire, that's okay too, but find any way you can to reframe your focus from "Why Me?" to something more motivational.

Through my own understanding of God and meaning in the universe, I began to explore the idea of forgiving the person responsible for my new life. Think about that for a minute. Is that an incredibly hard thing to do? Yes. Could I have falsely proclaimed forgiveness but continued to harbor a sense of anger and bitterness toward him? Absolutely. It was only through a seriously introspective look at faith, meaning, purpose, and an honest desire to feel better mentally and physically that I was able to be a truly forgiving person.

Finding forgiveness for the person who injured me was one of the most difficult things I've ever done, but it was completely worth it. Through understanding, spirituality, or your own logical deduction, find the place within your heart that allows you to forgive whomever is responsible for where you are today. Once you embrace that action, your potential for healing will open like a spring flower in full bloom.

Recommended Resource

Motivational author and founder of Hay House Publishing, Louise Hay published several wonderful books on faith and forgiveness. Worthy of particular mention is *You Can Heal Your Life*. Examine her full library of works to learn everything you can about her refreshing views on the interconnected-ness between body, mind, and spirit.

While reexamining my faith, I saw an advertisement for a Christian rock band (Third Day) that was playing a live show at a local church. With a lot of time on my hands and some amends to make with my family, I decided that taking my young kids to see the show would be a fun way to spend time together. Coincidentally that same band was playing on a CD in my brother Phil's car just days before while visiting my rapidly declining father with pancreatic cancer.

That night proved to be a defining moment in my recovery. When we got to the church, the air felt intense with inspiration; it was so different from everything I had experienced since my injury. A large number of people had gathered with the same idea in mind; they wanted to see a reason to feel better. They wanted to hear a message of hope and share in a unified feeling of peace, love, and motivation.

For years at that point, nothing had moved me in such a positive way. When the music played and the crowd got into it, I felt like I was in a place where I belonged for the first time in years. Perhaps most importantly, I felt motivated to do better.

My kids and I enjoyed the entire show. We shared a special night together as a family, and I felt empowered to get better like never before. When I got home, I felt determined to not let this emotion fade away overnight. With a renewed faith in my understanding of God and a newfound forgiveness in my heart, I was finally ready to heal.

That was the real beginning of my spiritual journey that had begun nearly thirty years earlier by great parents with great intentions who were just a bit too inconsistent for me. My brother Phil was also greatly influential in my journey and I am deeply and forever grateful for that. I married a Catholic girl and that helped too!

TIPS FOR BETTER SLEEP

To kick-start my healing process, I knew I had to sleep better. Sleep is an incredibly important aspect of a healthy life. It allows the body to power down and restore energy overnight. Quality sleep is like a charger for a battery. Without it, healthy individuals operate at far less capacity and efficiency. Trauma victims have the same problems with an additional difficulty, which is that the body can't heal properly. Without quality sleep, your recovery process will be severely delayed and possibly never reach its full potential.

Sleeping well was a problem for me before my injury. I think it is genetic for me. My younger brother Phil reminded me recently that our father, Phil, would be up at three o'clock in the morning cooking pork chops, steak, and shrimp. I inherited that "disease" and often found myself up at the same time, wondering why I couldn't sleep and feeling like I needed to "do something." Remember, my crash occurred in the middle of the night while moving my watercraft.

Afterward, it became a beast of burden, and I knew that had to change. Without proper rest, it's almost impossible to effectively manage the physical and psychological complications from pain.

Shortly after grasping forgiveness from my Bible readings, I developed a stronger relationship with my understanding of God. One night, I placed my faith in God to help me find a comfortable position in which I could at last get some much-needed sleep. Until that point, no matter which way I had tossed or turned, my pain alerted me of its presence. I tried to deny it on my left side, my right, my back, and my stomach, but that was no answer. Denial only made the pain speak louder.

Adults—whether victims of trauma or not—are recommended to get somewhere between six and eight hours of sleep per day. Your nighttime routine and environment should be customized to enable relaxation and sleeping. A comfortable mattress and pillow should be priority one.

For me, an adjustable bed frame with a slightly raised head and foot, that provided a gentle vibration, was helpful. There are several other types of mattresses and sleep aids that also promote better rest. Perform due diligence online or in person to see what works best for you.

Remain well hydrated during the day and avoid caffeine at night. Keep your bedroom dark and cool at bedtime, and stick to a regular sleep and wake-up schedule.

Natural sleep aids like melatonin are good for keeping your body's circadian rhythms in check. Cannabidiol (CBD) is another safe and effective option to not only help with sleep, but also to act as a mild but effective pain reliever. Many patients I've known have enjoyed great success using medical marijuana to treat pain.

Delta-8

At the time of this writing there is a product called Delta-8. I suggest you look into it if you struggle with sleep.

Delta-8 is legal and sold over the counter without any need for a medical marijuana card. Delta-8-Tetrahydrocannabinol (Delta-8-THC, Δ8-THC) is a psychoactive cannabinoid found in the cannabis plant. It is an isomer of Delta-9-Tetrahydrocannabinol (Delta-9-THC, Δ9-THC), the compound commonly known as THC. Delta-8-THC has antiemetic, anxiolytic, orexigenic, analgesic, and neuroprotective properties.

CBD and medical marijuana are good alternatives to hardcore narcotics like oxycodone or fentanyl (which can help, but also cause harm). Extreme caution should be exercised when taking these drugs on a regular basis. They are designed to treat acute pain, not chronic. When used over a prolonged period of time, narcotics can have highly undesirable side effects, addiction being chief among them. Another one is severe constipation, which can add substantially to a person's level of discomfort and emotional angst.

Narcotics in the Life Care Plan

Life care planners need to decide if they should include narcotics into the life care plan. When used long-term, their propensity for addiction and other problems presents quite a dilemma. If the patient has been on narcotics for several years and they're the only thing that has helped them manage their pain, it's hard not to recommend their usage. Careful evaluation must be analyzed to decide what the best course of action is for each patient.

Work with your care team to create strategies that will enable you to have a good night's sleep. Remember what I say all the time— documentation, rehabilitation, and restoration. Restoration requires restorative sleep!

Do whatever you need to do to get restorative sleep. If you need a prescription or technology-based aid, tell your doctor, work with your insurance company, and explain the necessity of this to your life care planner.

Your doctor may be able to write a prescription that helps, your insurance company may cover an adjustable bed or another device, and your life care planner may be able to put the pieces in place that ensure a decent night's rest is paid for throughout your lifetime.

Sleeping with PTSD

PTSD is a common problem for trauma victims with sleep disturbances. If you suffer from PTSD and are experiencing nightmares or startling wake-ups on a regular basis, get to a trauma psychologist as soon as possible. PTSD isn't a brain disorder; it's your body repeatedly reliving your traumatic event.

If you require a psychologist for ongoing treatment of PTSD or anything else, your life care planner will need to account for that. Do whatever it takes to get the help you need and that will lead to more restful evenings.

GETTING TO THANK YOU

With forgiveness in my heart and a more rested body and mind, I finally felt ready to make a vow to react differently to the next stabbing pain I felt in my chest or back. Essentially, I extended forgiveness into gratitude. Instead of thinking "Why me?" or "Screw You!" every time that pain surfaced, I said "Thank you."

I know that an expression of gratitude may sound strange, difficult, and downright ridiculous (especially when it is likely that someone's negligence or stupidity caused your dilemma), but it put me in an immensely better state of mind.

By saying "thank you" to the pain, I acknowledged that I was in my current situation for a reason. Whatever higher power exists in the universe, the "God of my understanding," they or it were trying to tell me something. I could not deny the presence of my pain, but I could control the meaning of what it was doing to me.

The pain was signaling me to contemplate all of those sixteen-hour workdays I had toiled through as a doctor. I would recall all of those times I wished things were different, and focus on the fact that now I didn't have to work so long, so hard, and so often. When I really thought about it, the universe gave me exactly what I had wished for. It was using pain to tell me that I needed to change something in my life.

Before my injury, I was heading down a slow but definite path of destruction with my marriage. Initially, the accident accelerated that process. Now, I had the chance to recognize where I had gone wrong and to reconcile the mistakes I had made with my wife and family, both before and after my injury.

Without my pain, I likely would have never realized the destructive path I was walking with my family. For that, I was truly grateful. Getting to "thank you" was a difficult process, but the mental refresh that gratitude gave me was well worth it. It would be disingenuous at best for me to say, however, that the physical pain itself was better because of the gratitude; it was still there. However, that peace of mind allowed me to manage the pain better and enabled me to focus on healing. *Enter in pieces, depart in peace.*

FORGIVENESS AND GRATITUDE

Until that point, I had already seen several excellent physicians, who had all told me some version of the same thing. "Santo, you're already at the optimal recovery point for your injury. Your pain is as good as it's going to get."

It was shortly after that when I met with a very special mentor, the only billionaire I had actually known, Charles "Red" Scott. We met in the nineties during a business conference in Tampa that was attended by over a thousand business leaders. He singled me out and we became friends. Later, he mentored me for several years. During dinner at this private dinner club in Atlanta, he said to me, "Doctor, heal thyself." I took *everything* Mr. Scott said to heart, but I especially listened to that admonition.

Shortly after my psychological reboot and new focus on forgiveness and gratitude, I pored through numerous listings of pain management professionals, looking for a superstar in the craft. Surely, somewhere in the world existed the Michael Jordan of pain management. That's when I found and referred myself to a doctor named Brian Chevis James, MD.

When I walked into Brian's office for the first time, I had already decided that my pain was *not* going to control me any longer. I was committed to taking control of my life once again. So, whatever benefit he could provide was fine in my mind. If he could take my pain from a nine to a seven and a half, I would take it.

Brian didn't recommend any super advanced treatment. His plan was to administer an RFA (radio frequency ablation) to the area that had been injected with novocaine and steroids earlier, only producing short-term relief.

Somehow, the results with Brian's technique were miraculous. Under his care, I went into pre-op, blinked my eyes, and the procedure was done. I looked up, saw Brian, and asked him, "When are we getting started?"

He laughed and replied, "We're done."

That's when I realized that not only was the procedure done, but so was my pain. I said, "Brian, you did it! My pain is gone!"

He laughed again and told me, "No, it's just temporary. I'll see you next week for a follow-up."

Brian was massively underselling his work. The pain never came back and, somehow, I knew it wouldn't right away. His procedure was a different experience than all of the other injections I had previously undergone.

"Brian, you healed me," I insisted. "The pain is not coming back. I'm certain of that."

He didn't believe me. But next week came and I had no pain. The week after that arrived, and I still had no pain. Next month—no pain. Years later—no pain. Today—still no pain! Only now, however, when I am tense or in a stressful situation do I get "twinges" in that exact area, and it reminds me to go back to the beginning of this journey, take a deep breath, and give thanks.

I don't often share this story with my patients, because I can't promise that they'll have the same result I did. Similarly I can't promise that your pain will disappear with a single treatment. However, I can, beyond a shadow of a doubt, honestly say that *less pain is possible*. I've lived that reality and I've seen it in other patients as well.

Once in a while, the pain nudges me; it usually coincides with an activity I don't like. Somehow the psychological overlaps with the physical in that way. Muscles have memory and we often say, "Your issues are in your tissues."

Occasionally, the pain will start to flare up when I'm talking with a person who is acting aggressively or being difficult. I also hate paying bills, so the pain often surfaces when I'm doing that as well.

Whenever my pain reminds me that it's still there, I stop whatever I'm doing. I lie down on the floor and I reframe my thinking. I start to think about where my mindset was before the pain arrived. Almost always, I realize that the pain resurfaced because my old mindset resurfaced. I became consumed with how much I disliked someone's attitude or how I loathed paying bills, which reactivated the pain signals. Eventually, I accept why the pain is there, I say, "Thank you," and I allow it to go away.

That might not be the exact experience you have, but the point is that we all have the power to modulate our pain when we decide to regain control of it.

Be curious about the healing power within your own mind. Look into resources about your body's healing power. Investigate your mindset and spirituality, and search globally for the best specialists and physicians qualified to help you.

Honestly assess your thoughts. Are you focused on anger, bitterness, and frustration? If so, I understand. That's where most of my thoughts were for *several years* after my injury. My understanding of forgiveness and gratitude did not happen overnight. Regrettably, it took far too long, and I wasted so much time.

Transform those thoughts and find forgiveness for whatever or whomever caused your injury. Become grateful—as difficult as it may seem—and you'll take a big step out of the darkness and into a healing light.

Getting from "Why me?" to "Thank you" is a major step in the right direction to your healing process. Once you achieve that state of mind, the chance for much better days will become a glowing light at the end of a dark tunnel.

Chapter 7

Vocational Issues:
Your Dream Job or Just a Job?

*"However difficult life may seem,
there is always something you can
do and succeed at."*

—Stephen Hawking (scientist)

Years ago, I treated a patient who was involved in not one or two but three serious motor vehicle accidents. Her name was Susanna, and she was an appellate attorney with an impeccable track record. She was smart, savvy, and loved helping people. Practicing law was a big part of her identity.

Susanna was badly injured in each of the three collisions. It was the third one, however, that resulted in a traumatic brain injury and affected her cognitive ability. Susanna was also a fighter, so she didn't give up easily. She hung on to her ability to effectively practice law for a long time.

Eventually, Susanna realized that she was still able to handle some of the work associated with litigation but struggled mightily with running an office, managing staff, writing briefs, dealing with trust accounts, and some of the other operations-related tasks of her practice. In the end, she decided the entirety of the situation was too much to handle and she walked away from her practice.

Fortunately, Susanna had built an excellent team around her personal injury case. I was her treating physician and life care planner, and she had excellent providers and attorneys as well. Together, we were able to achieve a settlement for Susanna that enabled her to make the transition from high-powered appellate attorney to a whole new life, one she always dreamed of but never before acted upon. Susanna exemplifies another sterling example of a silver lining to trauma. In this case, her injuries provided the catalyst for many positive life changes.

Again, trauma-related pain could be sending a message. For me, that pain was telling me to work less, appreciate my relationships more, and spend extended time with my family. Once I listened to what my pain was saying, I was able to make positive changes and begin the healing process.

In Susanna's case, the first accident may have been a not-so-gentle message that she should explore different avenues in life. The second crash may have been a firm reminder. The third accident that affected her cognitive ability was a definitive statement from pain that it was time for her to discover new ways to get more out of life.

Prior to her injury, Susanna had a passion for many things besides work. She loved to dance, travel, and write. Yet, she never acted on any of those things. She was too busy with her practice and helping others with their legal issues. She was also a go-getter type, fiercely competitive, and even posttrauma, maintained a high intellect that begged for an outlet.

A TBI is difficult for anyone to cope with, but for someone with Susanna's drive and fervor for life, the frustration can become overwhelming . . . unless they do something about it. That's why Susanna took action.

After learning about Susanna's non-law-related interests, there was one no-brainer activity that I prescribed as her rehab physician—dancing. Competitive ballroom dancing. Really hard stuff for anyone, especially someone with physical and cognitive impairments. But that is exactly what Susanna needed.

If the patient's physical abilities allow it, dance is beneficial to anyone's recovery process. It helps not only from a physiological perspective, but from a psychological one as well. Dancing is a creative outlet that feeds the body and mind.

Susanna took to the dance floor like a natural. It was like she was meant to appear on *Dancing with the Stars.* Watching her glide gracefully across the ballroom floor gave the impression dancing was a talent that had lain dormant within Susanna throughout her pretrauma lifetime.

At first, she danced for rehab and fun. Later on, her desire to be the best she could be surfaced, and it was quite impressive to witness. Once Susanna felt comfortable enough with her abilities, she became a competitive dancer. In fact, Susanna performed especially well in the tango and ballroom competitions.

When dancing worked out so well, Susanna explored other activities she always wanted to embrace but never had the time to try. She traveled to exotic destinations and wrote about her experiences. Susanna was successful before and after her injuries, but posttrauma her life actually became more diverse, colorful, and perhaps satisfying.

Because one of the things she liked most about practicing law was helping people, she didn't totally abandon her talent to act effectively as legal counsel. Instead, she adapted her role to better suit her new life.

Posttrauma, Susanna developed a new practice focused on client advocacy, where she helped people find the right attorneys for their particular case. This allowed her to continue working in the industry in which she'd had so much success, but without the enormous stress and anxiety she had thanks to the scope of her previous practice. Plus, it still allowed her the indulgences of life's finer things like dancing, traveling, and writing, among other activities.

Susanna went from the purely analytical business world of appellate law to the limitless possibilities of a creative existence, where she expressed herself more freely.

If you take anything from this book, understand the hope that Susanna's story symbolizes. Understand what is possible after trauma. If you felt like your life was limited by your previous career, or like your job was *just a job* and you didn't love it, this might just be your chance to make the change to something completely different and incredibly rewarding.

THE VOCATIONAL EVALUATION

In most life care plans, a vocational evaluation will be performed to account for damages related to lost earning capacity. This can comprise a large portion of the total claim.

> Personal injury cases are not the only situations in
> which a vocational evaluation is performed. They
> are also used in cases involving medical malpractice,
> product liability, wrongful termination, discrimina-
> tion, and even matrimonial litigation.

When I'm brought in to create a life care plan, one of the first things I talk about with the attorney is hiring a vocational expert. The client's medical provider will then work with the vocational expert to lay down the foundation of work restrictions and evaluate the person's lost earnings accordingly.

A vocational evaluation will use a battery of tests specifically geared to assess a patient's ability to work. It will test for memory, intelligence, aptitude, and more. Scores from each of these exams will be taken into account to provide an overall recommendation for the client's abilities.

The vocational evaluation is separate from the life care plan, but the two work together, hand in hand. In tandem, the two professionals will look at medical records and speak with treatment providers to determine a dollar figure that accounts for a patient's lost earning capacity based on several factors. They'll

come to an agreement on employer liability, residual employ-
ability, and future earning capacity. Further, they'll examine
the skills the patient has been able to retain and determine if
it's possible to rebuild lost function. If retraining is an option,
they'll look into that as well.

Use the life care plan as a tool to construct your vocational future.
Whether it's rebuilding your lifelong work or a totally divergent
career path, the life care plan can provide invaluable information and resources to get you back to work . . . somewhere.

Of course, two separate dollar figures are taken into consider-
ation regarding the vocational issues of a personal injury case.
First, there's lost earnings, which accounts for missed time
from work. Lost earnings are easily calculated by multiplying
your rate of pay by how much time was missed due to injury.

The more complex issue is lost earnings capacity, which con-
cerns lost future income. Many factors go into this assessment.
Current skillset, education level, job experience, performance
history, and other variables all need to be accounted for to arrive
at an accurate estimate.

This situation becomes even more complicated when evaluating the lost earning capacity of a child, where there is no
performance history or previous experience to factor into the
equation. Instead, the vocational expert and life care planner

will need to look at socioeconomic background, parent education, and the educational capacity of the child as well as their overall cognitive ability.

SILVER LININGS

Many people consider work to be more than simply a means of putting food on the table, paying the mortgage, and providing adequate clothing for the kids. Sure, those things are important, but for many of us, work plays a much larger role in our lives; it defines who we are.

When trauma-related disability or pain takes that away, intense emotional struggles may follow, and even dominate our lives. Fear, anxiety, and depression can loom large when our normal routine is disrupted so significantly. Some of us might feel as if we've lost our identity.

When our capacity to earn a living is taken away, it affects much more than lost income. In a way, being unable to perform our jobs can lessen our value of ourselves. As dysfunctional and incorrect as that mindset might be, it's part of our societal upbringing to associate a certain sense of our value with the work we do.

Athletes, in particular, struggle with posttrauma career

direction. Many times, their future is tied into what they can do with their bodies. They've established a workout routine and have accumulated tens of thousands of hours in practicing their chosen sport. *What happens once their body can no longer respond the way it always has?*

If you've created a life around your athleticism or physical abilities, honestly assess whether or not your body has a good chance of recovering to the point that will allow you to continue working as you were before. If not, other vocations will always be there for you to pursue. Attack that new career path with newfound enthusiasm to be great at it.

Of course, you may have to make the change from a physical career to one that focuses more on intellectually focused skills and abilities. This new life may earn more or less income, but if you discover something you love to do, you'll be far happier regardless. Besides, if you have a life care plan in place, financial resources won't be a concern like they were before your injury anyway.

> Whether you're an athlete, schoolteacher, firefighter, accountant, dog trainer, or anything else, with forgiveness and gratitude at the forefront of your approach, there is always something else you can do.

You could go from being a truck driver to an accountant or vice versa. If you're in a situation where your livelihood is in jeopardy due to a traumatic injury, ask yourself the following question: did you *love* your job? If the answer is no or not really, now is the time to pursue that silver lining.

LOCKED-IN AND LIVING WITH PURPOSE

Never *assume* your injury is too restrictive to allow you to work. There are countless ways to be productive in life. Consider the true story of Jean-Dominique Bauby, which I consider to be the most inspirational and amazing account I've ever heard about overcoming extreme challenges to live with purpose.

Bauby was a French author and journalist who wrote and edited for *Elle* magazine. Tragically, at forty-three years old, Bauby experienced a rare, major stroke in his brain stem. Twenty days later, he awoke in a hospital bed, fully aware of his surroundings but unable to communicate or move a muscle, except for his left eye. He could blink that eye and move it side to side and up and down, but nothing else.

The condition is called locked-in syndrome. It occurs when patients can think, see, and hear the world around them. They cannot, however, talk or move at all, except for the muscles in their eyes. In the rarest of cases, some patients can't even do that.

In Bauby's case, he refused to admit defeat. He had a story to tell and *nothing*—I mean *nothing*—was going to stop him from telling it.

Although he could only move one eye, Bauby decided early in his posttrauma life to make the most of that ability. With the aid of an amanuensis (literary assistant), Bauby used his eye to dictate letters of the French alphabet. Bauby blinked his eye or moved it in certain patterns, signaling his assistant to write down corresponding letters that formed words, sentences, paragraphs, and eventually, a bestselling 144-page book called *The Diving Bell and the Butterfly.*

The book is not only an amazing accomplishment of the human spirit, but also a compelling and inspiring work that stands alone in its literary excellence. Any writer of any capacity would be proud to have produced such a work of impact and meaning.

Fate seemed to be aligned with Bauby's mission. Two days after the book was published, he succumbed to complications of pneumonia and somewhat mercifully passed away. It's as if God, the universe, or life itself wanted to wait for Bauby to tell his story.

Bauby's achievement tells us that no matter what your situation is, you have the ability to do something that will add purpose to your life.

Now, take some time to think about what you want to do and how you can do it. Use the power of your mind, take advantage of whatever physical abilities you have, and blink if you need to, but live with purpose.

Recommended Resource

The Diving Bell and the Butterfly by Jean-Dominique Bauby.

OPPORTUNITY KNOCKS

To make an accurate assessment of your vocational abilities, establish and maintain excellent communication with your treatment team. Confer with them to determine the reality of your situation. Then, think about what *you* believe to be possible.

If you're unable to get back to work now, use your free time to think about your future. You might consider how you get back to work, how you change careers, or focus solely on recovery.

The path you choose doesn't matter, but you likely now have the free time you always wanted to think about your future. Understand the opportunity you have today and use it wisely.

Consider a number of factors when evaluating your ability to work now and later. It's not as simple as waiting for your wounds to heal. Ask yourself some questions:

- Has your cognitive ability been impaired?

- How much will chronic pain affect your ability to work?

- What kind of toll will the lack of sleep that often accompanies injury have on your job performance?

- Will the medications you take impact your functionality at work?

Try to find and communicate with people who have already overcome physical, emotional, and cognitive challenges. Throughout your recovery process, you'll encounter people who have beaten trauma greater than yours. I, for instance, was inspired by many others who reached new heights after their injury, and that understanding played a large, inspirational role in my healing. Put the days of wishing for something different behind you, and concentrate instead on what you can still achieve. *Recognize the powerful resilience within you.*

Service Animals

Service animals can be a wonderful benefit for people who are managing trauma.

A few years after my injury, I purchased, raised, and trained two gorgeous Dobermans (Sorrento and Capri) that proved to be an invaluable part of my recovery. They were specially trained to detect my frustration level. Just by being around me, they could tell what my energy level was and help me when I needed it.

If you're struggling with your trauma—or even if you're just looking for a faithful companion—service animals can help in a variety of ways.

Chapter 8

Preparation for Litigation

"You never know how strong you are until being strong is your only choice."

—Bob Marley (singer)

It is the job of a plaintiff attorney to hire the life care planner *early* in the litigation process. That way, the life care plan can be written with ample time before any deposition or trial takes place. This is beneficial because it lets both sides of the litigation know what the facts are. Hopefully, this facilitates a situation where you receive financial resources without the need for a courtroom appearance.

THE PURPOSEFUL PERSONAL PLANNER

If a trial does become necessary, clarity about the facts will enable the truth to emerge. As such, you (as the plaintiff) will want to keep track of dates and times noteworthy events occurred, the medications you take, how they affected you, what your pain levels were like, physician appointments, and what they did during the appointments.

The best way I know to ensure clarity is to consistently log entries into a personal planner, documenting the patients, injury, treatment, and recovery. This takes the guesswork out of trying to recall facts about a certain day many years later. The personal planner is a perfect accompaniment to the life care plan in a courtroom.

In the digital age, it's easy to rely on an app for everything. Many people have abandoned the idea of keeping a personal planner in favor of electronic note-taking. If that works for you, great. My experience, however, is that the written word and physical copy provides a much more tangible, helpful record of the facts. I believe in this old-fashioned way of record keeping so much for my patients that each one of them receives a BMG (BiFulco Medical Group) daily planner when I first meet with them. I tell them to log their daily observations meticulously because not only will it provide the facts in a court of law, but it's also an excellent way for them to track their own progress.

DEPOSITION

The deposition process is part of what's called the discovery phase of the case. This is when all the facts are put on the table, so both parties know how far apart they are on any potential settlement agreement.

An inquiry takes place on the date of deposition by the plaintiff's legal team and the defense counsel. It usually occurs in a closed conference room, around a table with all stakeholders present. The purpose is to discover all of the facts known or unknown by the witness in an effort to come to a settlement so that a trial won't be necessary.

If attempts to settle out of court are unsuccessful, courtroom testimony (a.k.a. a trial) in front of a judge and jury becomes necessary.

About 50 percent of the trauma cases I've been involved with have included a deposition. If the two parties are reasonably close in terms of damages, which happens most of the time, a trial can be avoided. In rare cases—probably about 5 percent of the time—the two parties are so far apart in their dollar figures that a trial becomes unavoidable.

Avoiding trial is an appealing end result for both sides because a lot of resources go into preparing for a court date. Experts must be located and secured, extensive research must be performed, and a great deal of stress is involved for all stakeholders. Legal services alone are quite expensive. Investment of all these resources amounts to considerable risk for the plaintiff and defense, which makes a settlement much more appealing in almost every situation.

Even after all the facts are on the table and both sides understand what's at stake if litigation goes to trial, tough negotiations may still ensue. If both sides feel justified in their position, a settlement may not be possible. However, even among the most stubborn of arbitration, a settlement occurs at some point, often in the final days before trial—occasionally the previous night or even just a few hours before the date.

If a trial becomes unavoidable, it's important to know that there are two aspects of the litigation process—liability and damages.

Liability is the determination of fault for the incident. It is the realm of the attorneys, the expert witnesses, judge, and jury to figure out who, if anybody, is liable. Was there negligence? Was a building code ignored? Did somebody not do their job correctly? As the injured party, you shouldn't focus your energy on this side of litigation. It's mostly out of your control, so let the people who get paid to sort this out do their jobs.

TRIAL PREPARATION

Transparency is key in any pending litigation. Just be yourself and answer any questions honestly and to the best of your ability. Later on, it will look good to the future decision makers like judges and juries (the trier of fact) if you've been up front from the beginning.

Your best bet (as the plaintiff) during the litigation process is to assume that every note, comment, action, and thought will come forward in a trial setting. Don't hide anything, because expert attorneys and other stakeholders will do their homework to uncover every bit of information on which they can get their hands.

Once you walk into a courtroom in a trial setting, you never know who the jurors are. How you conduct yourself in front of this group of strangers is crucial to the outcome of your case. You want to dress properly, use positive language, don't appear defensive, and even inject a spot of humor occasionally if possible. Above all, be transparent, hide nothing, and state all the facts.

When you appear in a courtroom, remember to take every action seriously. You never know who is watching. There are jurors present, a bailiff, a judge, legal assistants, defense counsel, and countless others who all have a job to do and will be carefully watching your reactions. You don't want to be caught off guard in front of any of them because you never know what kind of impact it will have. Understand that every aspect of the proceedings is a serious matter and you need to treat them as such. Everything you say and do will be called into question and highlighted. Don't take anything personally, but take it all seriously.

DAMAGES

Instead of focusing your efforts on the things you can't control, think about how to restore yourself to health. Whether or not liability is determined to be in your favor, you still need to know how to get better; you'll still need to follow your roadmap to recovery.

Once liability is determined, your legal team will move on to identify the damages you should receive to make yourself whole again, financially speaking. Damages are the monetary value associated with your injury. A life care planner can be especially helpful in this part of your case. In fact, this is where the life care plan itself is most useful.

A PERSONAL INJURY TRIAL CASE STUDY

In the first year of my medical practice as a rehabilitation physician, I got a call from a high-profile, nationally recognized attorney, Greta Van Susteren. She asked if I would be the treating physician for a client of hers. More than that, she explained that accepting the role would likely require me to provide expert testimony in his case at some point as well.

The client was a young man who lived in Michigan. He was recently married and needed to get some brake work done on his vehicle. Shortly after leaving the repair shop, he merged onto a local highway and his brakes failed. The result was a multitrauma accident with a brain injury—for a young man with a new wife and his entire life in front of him.

By the time I received the phone call, the client had moved his residence to a home converted into a rehabilitation facility in Clearwater, Florida. It was literally walking distance from my office and the hospital (Morton Plant), where I was the director of the department of rehabilitation.

About a month prior, I had completed the purchase of a second location for my practice in the same city. So, logistically, accepting the role of his rehabilitation physician made sense.

As part of this patient's treatment, I made monthly visits to his place in Clearwater for about eighteen months. During these visits, I asked him questions, monitored his progress, and continued to develop plans for his future care.

The vast majority of personal injury cases end in a settlement, but once in a while, the two sides are too far apart to reach a mutual agreement without a court of law administering a resolution. That was the situation in this case. The plaintiff's legal team and the defense were miles apart in the dollar figure this young man required for his injuries.

His trial took place in the middle of winter in Lapeer, Michigan. I had no idea what to expect when I arrived. This was one of the first times I had ever provided expert testimony in a litigation case, so I wanted to do everything to the best of my ability. It was about more than just performing my job to a level of excellence. I also wanted to do right by this young man who had his life tragically altered from one bad brake job.

Greta had secured a set of local hotel rooms as her pretrial setting for the night before my court appearance. When I showed up to prepare for my testimony, she and her staff spent several hours asking me questions that they expected the defense to present the next day. This was an invaluable experience that gave me a crash course in the world of injury litigation. The evening was tough because, at times, I wasn't sure how to answer, but thankfully, I had the attorney and her team to help me through it, so I was ready for those difficult exchanges when the trial took place the next day.

When I took the stand, my direct examination covered my qualifications, detailed my assessment of the patient, and requested the facts about my corresponding treatment of this patient's injury. That part was a piece of cake.

After lunch break, the cross-examination from the defense team began. This was a vastly different experience from the line of questioning that the client's legal team provided, and it took much longer. The entire process was no piece of cake; it was a bitter, inedible chunk of reality.

The defense dissected my training, experience, and credentials. They didn't mention the actual case much at all; it was mostly about me. Their intent was to discredit me as a reputable source, but it didn't work.

My training as a resident proved valuable at that time. I was learning under an attending physician who had a teaching method that involved asking a barrage of questions on every lesson. Over several weeks, this constant questioning made me and the other students incredibly well-prepared to react *in the moment* with good decisions. I didn't realize it then, but that experience served me incredibly well in this trial setting.

Back then, I was not yet a life care planner, but taking part in this experience versed me on the types of care a patient could require over a lifetime. It accustomed me to providing medical opinions based on a patient's projected long-term care.

The defense went into the painstaking details of my experience with the plaintiff. They asked me about every visit, and wanted to know who was present for the examinations, what we did, the things we talked about, and every other detail that could be extracted.

Because the plaintiff's team was so well prepared and thorough in their litigation preparation, that young man was able to receive a large ruling for damages. Still, I can't help but wonder how much smoother the life care plan would have made things for him, how much grief it might have saved, how much quicker the situation would have resolved, if it would have enabled a settlement rather than force a trial, or if he would have been given an even larger amount of damages.

Fortunately, if you're reading this, you won't have any thoughts of regret pertaining to any of those unanswered questions. You'll know all about the importance of preparing a life care plan as soon as possible.

CONCLUSION

"Keep some room in your heart
for the unimaginable."

—Mary Oliver (poet)

I hope this book has given you some clarity on what some of your options are. If you or someone close to you is in pain or has suffered a serious injury or catastrophic, chronic, disabling condition, or you're a plaintiff or defense attorney, please listen carefully to what I am about to tell you. It will not be a waste of your valuable time, and I promise you that what you're about to learn can have a significant positive effect on you or the folks that you represent.

I'm an American born and trained physician, a medical doctor who specializes in physical medicine and rehabilitation—a specialty also known as physiatry (fizz-eye-at-tree)—as well as life care planning.

A physiatrist is a doctor who is trained in physical rehabilitation, orthopedic medicine, neurology, and neurological rehabilitation—all manners of trauma care and pain management. I am now in my thirty-first year of private practice. I have advanced training in pediatric and adult brain injuries, spinal cord injuries, amputations, pain management for herniated discs, spinal injuries such as paraplegia and quadriplegia, as well as burns, strokes, cerebral vascular accidents, heavy-metal toxicity, autism, disability evaluations, birth injuries, and life care planning.

I am a trained and experienced physician life care planner. I have authored hundreds of serious and catastrophic life care plans over the past decade. A life care plan is a communication tool. It is a comprehensive document or report that outlines the cost and type of future medical care and services an injured person will need now and for the remainder of their life. In other words, a care plan for life.

A life care plan is a time-tested and proven litigation and pre-litigation communication tool; however, it is also used outside the realm of litigation. I currently treat or have treated or have authored life care plans for all those conditions stated as well as many others. Common injuries for which I author life care plans include trucking, motorcycle, and auto accidents; medical malpractice injuries; product liability cases; premise liability cases; assaults such as gunshot wounds or other traumas; as well as wrongful death cases. I maintain an active current and clear license to practice medicine in the states of Florida and New York.

I'm routinely retained by both the plaintiff and defense firms. I've testified in person in federal and state courts in Florida, New York, California, Michigan, Virginia, and many states throughout the United States as well as Canada and Bermuda. My professional expert opinions have been accepted in state and federal courts throughout the United States.

I have founded and co-founded many medical practices and offices throughout West Central Florida and South Florida including medical rehabilitation clinics and a clinic for special needs children where my team and I utilized intensive physiotherapies and hyperbaric oxygen to treat their conditions. Through our clinic in South Florida, which I co-founded and was the medical director for, I was able to treat many brain-injured children from around the world.

I presently live and work in the Tampa Bay area with my wife of thirty-five years, who is a registered rehab nurse and also a wound care specialist, as well as my three adult children and my now eight-year-old granddaughter.

After more than thirty-one years of private practice, I remain passionate about what I do and compassionate towards every individual regardless of who retains me. I am blessed to still love what I do. I've been told that the reasons why folks choose me for their medical care or medical legal matters include my professionalism, my availability, my approachability, and my ability to communicate the facts, and the fact that I truly care about people.

To get more information on how to work directly with me and my team or to get started on your life care plan go to www. GetLifeCarePlan.com.

ACKNOWLEDGEMENTS

Thank you to Michael Mogill with Crisp Video Productions, founder and CEO of Crisp, the nation's number one law firm growth company. He's helped attorneys and he has help ME. He was the last one who suggested I write a book, so I did! He connected me with his publisher and the rest is history.

I want to sincerely thank my publishing manager, Jericho Westendorf, and my scribe, David Caissie.

ABOUT THE AUTHOR

Dr. BiFulco wears a few hats, depending on the time of day and the time of year. He is a believer, a leader, and a follower. A son and a father, a husband and a grandfather (Nano). He loves to go fast and slow down. He skis, dives, and occasionally pilots helicopters as a student pilot these days.

Dr. BiFulco is a licensed physician in the states of Florida and New York; Dr. BiFulco holds specialty training and certifications in interventional pain management, radio-frequency therapy, and intradiscal therapy. Dr. BiFulco is licensed by the United States Drug Enforcement Agency to prescribe. Dr. BiFulco is a board-certified physician life care planner.

Dr. BiFulco's professional career includes decades of clinical practice, treating thousands of patients with all manner of acute, chronic, and catastrophic injuries and illnesses. Dr. BiFulco has occupied numerous medical directorships and medically oriented advisorship positions. As a medical doctor/entrepreneur, Dr. BiFulco founded and managed successful clinical practices and medical centers.

Dr. BiFulco's professional associations include the American Academy of Physical Medicine and Rehabilitation, the American Medical Association, the National Association of Disability Evaluating Professionals, the International Association for Rehabilitation Professionals, the Society for Pain and Practice Management, International Association of Rehabilitation Professionals, the International Symposium of Life Care Planning, and others. Dr. BiFulco is a certified diplomate of the National Board of Medical Examiners and of the Center for Advanced Medicine and Clinical Research.